Ready To Own a Salon?

10 Things You Should Know!

CHAPTER 1

WELCOME

Congratulations on your new adventure. Deciding to be your own boss and perhaps a leader to others is a bold move to be commended.

Calling the shots and deciding how your business grows and is profitable takes commitment, time, and determination to succeed.

It is important to note; success is achieved by overcoming failure. One must learn to understand why something is not working while also recognizing the behavior. Should failures begin to repeat themselves, stop, and take a moment to reflect. Frequent frustration can lead to incorrect decision-making; be aware of your approach to choices.

The real success of a business is defined in itself. This statement is to say, be careful of judging your success against others. Indeed, it is easy to feel like a failure compared to Warren Buffett or Mark Cuban, but you should understand that these people achieved their successes by never quitting and making many judgment errors. They became successful by learning everything about their business they could, researching opportunities, surrounding themselves with people in the know, and finally recognizing how to recover when a failure occurred. They didn't succeed by comparing their value to other successful people; they learned from other successful people.

In my thirty-five years plus in the business world, I have learned something new daily. The world continues to grow and change, and one must adapt to daily alterations to continue growing. With that in mind, be clear about your core values and how you choose to be perceived.

While interviewing people in the industry, as case studies for this book, I found it interesting that I could apply virtue characteristics to each of them. This suggests that each of us reveals our true selves through how we operate our business.

One participant was, what I like to call, Cheeky. An English term used to define someone who is "B*old, brash, and a bit rude, but also maybe a little playful and amusing*." Another one struck me as a Wobbler.

A Wobbler is a legal term in California, meaning a case can be a misdemeanor or a felony, depending on how it is prosecuted. In this case, the Wobbler likes to play on each side of the rules, depending on how it suits them. The third study, they were inquisitive. This can be an excellent quality but also get in the way of making decisions.

While reading this book, consider which of these you might be classified as. It is not vital beyond having the ability to self-evaluate. Self-reflection is critical to finding success.

My experience in coaching and guiding people toward success has taught me that each of us processes information differently. I assert that one must understand how one processes information, or else constantly feel a step behind the crowd.

Not everything you need to know will be included here; just as I learn something new every day, you will as well.

As Albert Einstein said,

"A person who never made a mistake never tried anything new!"

Good for you - you are trying something new, and you will undoubtedly have an adventure like none other.

Below are the case studies I reference from time to time.

Case Study #1: Angie.

Angie is a sole proprietor, she works as a lease tenant in a salon and has moved her business a few times. A single mother of two, she does her best to balance work life with home life. Being self-employed has served her well with the exception of having shared insurance cost for her family. Her biggest challenge in going it alone was her lack of business knowledge. During our interview, she said she never gave her taxes much thought until a letter from the IRS arrived inquiring where her quarterly filings were.

Study #2: Marcus.

Marcus set up his business as an S-Corp. With the help of a CPA, he received guidance on managing expenses and tracking revenue. He got off track when he opted to not operate a virtuous business. His omissions on business expenses would be caught by the IRS. Had he been forthcoming with his CPA, a review of his books would have revealed his expense to income ratios were not in line.

Study #3: Husband and wife team, Toni and Dan.

Dan and Toni opened a salon with employees as a partnership. This model was suggested by a family member as the best course of action. Dan has a full-time job which covers the family's expenses; Toni's income from dressing hair was supplemental to their overall income. Their chosen structure pushed them into a new tax bracket, ultimately reducing their take-home pay. They didn't use a CPA, and when they decided to divorce, their lack of having an attorney help set up the business created a whole new set of issues for them.

CHAPTER 2

OWNERSHIP TYPE

Laying out your business structure is a critical part of the process.

Knowing how you intend to track your finances and report the information to the government is paramount. The IRS will know if you are making money and being honest about how it is reported. Determining your business structure will keep the business intent clear and keep you out of a difficult situation.

The primary types of Business Structures that exist for IRS purposes are:

- ❖ Sole Proprietor

- ❖ Partnership

- ❖ Corporation

- ❖ S Corporation

- ❖ Limited Liability Company (LLC's)

There are reasons for each of them, and depending on your long-term business plans and revenue stream, you will need to find the one best suited for you. Each chapter within the book will tie back to how you establish your business initially.

Sole proprietor is exactly as it sounds; a single person who owns and operates a business; a business deemed *unincorporated*. It is, in effect, self-employment. This simply means you run things as you see fit and report your earnings through your personal income tax.

Partnership: A partnership is two or more people forming a business relationship. Each party contributes money, property, time, or skill and shares in the business' profits and losses.

Corporation: If you choose the corporation route, you will seek shareholders to invest in your company with money, property, or both; this is called capital stock. There are significant tax benefits for doing this. However, you must realize you are utilizing other people's money or property; you must answer to them for decisions made. Shareholders expect to get a return on their investment.

S-Corporation: S corporations are similar to the corporation dynamic listed above; the difference is that they pass corporate income, losses, deductions, and credits to their shareholders for tax purposes. The data is then reported on their personal income taxes. This avoids double taxation on corporate income. Like the corporation, stakeholders expect to see a return on their investment.

Limited Liability Company (LLC): this business structure varies State by State. This business filing is done within the State in most cases; each using various regulations to govern this status. The owners are *Members*, and may be an individual or a partnership. Generally, salons may be formed as an LLC, but this is a determination your CPA will evaluate.

Regardless of your chosen structure, remember you are now responsible for all taxation due. We will cover that in Chapter 7.

And yes, it is imperative that you have a lawyer and a CPA. This nominal cost invested now will reduce the risk of surprise expenses down the road.

Seek help from professionals who are in the know and not from your friends' experiences. While your network and the information they bring are valuable tools, they won't stand in court or with an auditor.

How do you decide what business model to use?

Hire a _____.

CHAPTER 3

WHO AM I?

Chapter 2 provided some fundamental insight into how you might want to structure your business with the help of a professional.

The rest of the book focuses on the three most common models for the salon industry. We will review the case studies to show examples of the impact of each.

The typical structures used for salons are:

- ❖ Sole Proprietor
- ❖ S-Corp
- ❖ Partnership

Keep in mind that this information is relevant regardless of whether you are leasing a station or starting a traditional salon. The business principles apply across the board; only the scale changes.

Sole proprietor is just another way to say self-employed. Most people leasing a station and operating a single chair without employees will fall into this category. Taxes fall into your standard filing each year but still require quarterly payments to the IRS; in essence, you are paying your taxes as you go. Just look at it like this; when you worked in other businesses, they held back your taxes before you received a paycheck; you are now doing this for yourself. Your CPA will help you determine how much to put away; this is a complicated calculation, and you want to avoid any penalties from the government. A lack of knowledge is not an excuse they will let you off the hook for. Depending on what you are paying your CPA, chances are the penalty from the IRS will be way more than the cost of an accountant.

I mentioned Angie earlier; she wasn't aware she needed to hold back taxes for quarterly payments. The end of the year came; she did her tax return and filed them. Angie was reasonably diligent in keeping up with expenses, and what her clients paid her every visit, she felt she was prepared for her submission to the tax authority.

Angie thought that by being self-employed, the rules were different for her. She lacked the understanding of how basic accounting principles applied. "I never wanted to be one of those people you see the commercial about - the ones who just didn't pay their taxes. You know, the woman crying on her rocking chair about how unfair the IRS was to her. I kept up with all my receipts and income to avoid being a commercial!"

Regardless of your chosen structure, money coming in and going out impact your business. Personal expenses like groceries or utilities for your home are not a part of the business. Although these costs are real and certainly reduce the amount of cash in your pocket, they don't affect your business income filing. On the other hand, your lease rent and utilities associated with where you perform your services must be tracked; they reduce your tax liability at the end of the year.

Look at Angie; at the end of one week, she had $1200 in her checking account. There was no distinguishing if this was personal or work-related. She paid her personal expenses of $300 and business expenses of $350; she thought she had $550 left over for whatever she wanted. She didn't.

We will come back to Angie later in the book; you will understand why she had less than she thought.

S-Corps are generally set up for multi-person salons. They can be set up for an individual as the Sole investor. There are many advantages to this, but I highly recommend not doing this without the help of a good CPA. The IRS highly scrutinizes these businesses; deductions and expenses are looked into in more detail because you are now receiving a salary from the corporation you have invested in. You may receive advice that you can reduce taxation this way due to how the money flows through the business; I strongly advise you to understand how this works. Don't be shy to ask your CPA for scenarios on your finances for year end.

Look at the model for Sole Proprietor and S-Corp. Determine which one will benefit you the most at the end of the year. Also, make sure to note the difference in accounting fees for both models.

Remember, your CPA is there to guide and offer advice; they are not your boss, so don't hesitate to ask questions and seek advice from multiple sources. If the business is a partnership of any kind, there may be advantages to filing for an S-Corp. I would caution that if there is only one of you, do your best to understand the impact on your business.

Marcus set up his business as an S-Corp on the advice of his CPA. He put a salary in place and every week paid himself from the company, put his taxes aside, wrote off his expenses, and by the time he was done, the *company* was losing money. He was reducing his personal income tax due to the structure of the business.

Sounds great, right?

The question to ask is, how does the business not have any money but still afford to pay his salary?

If there is money coming in, where did it all go? This is a play of hands, and while not necessarily illegal, it lends itself to a high level of scrutiny from auditors.

Marcus did not clearly understand the perception of having an S-Corp.

Partnerships are a standard business practice for the salon industry. People frequently combine different skill sets and assets to start a salon. This would be uncommon for a lease station but could be utilized if two people were looking to share a space and wanted equal control over the lease. My experience with this arrangement has been working with business people wanting to invest in a salon but not wanting day-to-day control over the main activities. Let's take Dan and Toni, he was a businessman (in this case, he also happened to be her husband), and she was a stylist. After working in a commission-based salon for ten years, they decided to open a place for her to work and employ others. They opted not to incorporate based on information provided by a family member, keeping the business as a partnership.

Life was good, they were in love, and Dan made enough money to cover their home expenses, so this should have been a sure thing.

What was not explained to them was the impact to their income now that they had a business in which he was investing.

Dan was an intelligent businessman; however, he had never owned his own business and wasn't well versed in the structure and taxation of a partnership.

"Two years into the salon being opened and massive losses due to a lack of knowing how to run the salon, we were on the edge of bankruptcy and divorce. We avoided bankruptcy but ruined the marriage."

Had they hired an attorney and CPA, they would have most likely made other choices that might have avoided their parting ways.

Before deciding how you want to set up your structure, think about all the aspects of life. I highly recommend making a Pros and Cons list to help assess what makes the most sense. If you are working with other people, have them make one of their own and compare notes. See if you are on the same page.

Should you look to obtain financing for your endeavor, this Pros/Cons list can be translated into a SWOT analysis a lender will ask for. Unless you have attended business school, don't try to build the analysis without help from someone who truly understands the goal and will challenge you on the input.

So Who Do You Want To Be?

☐ **Sole Proprietor**

☐ **S Corp**

☐ **Partnership**

CHAPTER 4

LOCATION

You have most likely heard the term Location, Location, Location. But how do you know if you are in a good spot?

Stop and look at who your customer is; who is your demographic audience?

In other words, who will be visiting your chair(s), and what is their primary form of transit?

If you live in an urban area with favorable mass transit, logic suggests you want to be near a transit stop.

On the flip side, if the town where your shop is located requires people to get around in their personal vehicle, you have to be sure plenty of parking spaces are readily available.

Do a little math and determine how many customers you expect to see daily. Think about how often they will "Come and go:" AKA Turn Over. If the primary service offered in your shop is haircuts, you will turn over a parking space approximately every thirty minutes. Whereas if your service menu is predominately chemical services, that parking space will be occupied for extended periods.

You need to ensure you have parking spaces for people to easily access your building; safely and with minimal inconvenience. Most people come to the salon by themselves, so plan one space for every service. Remember that some people will come early and leave late, the spot they utilize may not be open for your next customer when they arrive.

The logic suggests that the more chairs in the salon - the more parking spaces required. To make it simple, planning one-and-a-half space for every chair should provide ample parking for your patrons.

If you are a single-chair shop in a large group of single-chair shops; count the number of service spaces in the building and do the math.

You don't want to be short on parking spots on a busy Saturday and have a client possibly leave before their appointment due to a lack of parking.

Another aspect of your customer to think about; are they used to paying for parking? In some areas, parking is abundant and doesn't cost to use. If your customer has to pay for parking during their visit, be mindful of their expense. Perhaps offer that fee as part of your service, but most definitely, be very cognizant of their time. You don't want to waste their hard-earned money unintentionally.

Marcus had his parking well calculated; plenty of spaces were available front and back of his building. He calculated the need for the eight people in his shop which was located in a strip shopping center. He was surprised to learn that the bar next door took over the back parking lot after 4:00 PM every day. There was now a $5.00 fee for parking for any of his clients in the evening. He countered this by negotiating a deal with the bar to offer reduced-rate parking for salon customers until 8:00 PM. Great way to resolve the issue, and everyone in his shop enjoyed the rewards of his effort.

In Chapter 6: Making Money, we will dig more into the topic of what to charge to make money. What is essential to consider when choosing a location is what you can expect to charge people. Suppose you are in a swanky part of town or the trendiest new neighborhood, you can get away with charging more (and you should in order to be profitable). If you are in an area that is more settled and not as exciting, your price point will need to be lower.

I will caution you to be mindful of this when deciding where to locate your business, especially if you are moving your business. Angie moved her shop from an up-and-coming neighborhood to a lower-rent district.

Her thought was, "I would keep my pricing the same and be able to put more money in my pocket. I didn't realize some of my customers were opposed to the surroundings we had in Deep Ellum. In short, I lost a lot of my clients. In the area I was now located in, many of the locals could not afford my fees."

For Angie, this was a harsh lesson. She had expectations that her customers would follow her anywhere, and while some did, it took her a long time to rebuild her client base.

Toni and Dan had a different situation. Dan had the foresight to lease their space in an up-and-coming neighborhood. The salon with six chairs would easily cover the rent expenses and support their growing business. He had a great business plan set out for five years and signed the lease for five years, locking in their rental rate.

"The first sign of trouble was when the CAM fees increased significantly in year two. The building owners were making improvements to the property, which were important, but I had no say in what they spent, and my lease required I share in the expense and we couldn't afford to relocate."

For Dan and Toni, this quickly became an issue, and they had to adjust the salon's fee structure to offset the expense. They lost about 10% of their existing business when the pricing changed. The brutal hit for them was when their lease was up for renewal at the end of the five years.

"The original owners of the building sold the property, and when the lease came up for renewal, we had no relationship with the new landlord. He was happy to have us go and put another salon in the same place. And so began the marital discord."

As you have begun to notice, there are many variables to where you set your shop. Do your homework.

If you are leasing space within a salon, talk to the other renters in the shop (obviously when they are not with a client). Just like you would with an apartment or a house, check out the neighborhood, so to speak. Does the landlord take care of things quickly when there is an issue? Is there any evidence of unwanted behavior on the property? Get a sense that you will be comfortable before committing to your new location.

If you are setting up a multi-chair salon, talk to other tenants in the building, and find out if they have had any issues with building management or maintenance.

The last thing I highly recommend is to research the criminal records for the area. This will take a day of your time, but you may be shocked by what is going on nearby that you don't want to be associated with.

"We knew it was a party area - that was part of what working in this area was about - having fun and enjoying the scene around us. What we didn't know was the crack house behind us would bring us unwanted visitors to the salon." - Marcus.

Be mindful of where you are setting up your business. There will be things you don't like, but that is a part of life in business; use your pros/cons list.

"What can I live with?"

Decide what makes sense for the people you want to attract to your chair.

CHAPTER 5

SPACE

We are going to look at the different options for having a Space to work.

While it is essential to have enough room to perform your craft adequately, take into consideration the following:

- ❖ CAM's

- ❖ Supply Storage

- ❖ Product Display

- ❖ Dirty Laundry

- ❖ Shampoo Station

- ❖ Occupancy Certificate

These are fundamental parts of your business, whether going solo with one chair or partnering up in a more prominent location with multiple stylists.

Once you have finalized your business location, dig into the requirements for these categories before signing the lease.

Common Area Maintenance: Consider the space people use before entering your shop. Who is responsible for making sure it is kept clean and safe? In a situation where there are multiple shops under one roof, do you have any responsibilities to the common areas? If you lease a station in an open-air location (no walls separating your business from the others), who is responsible for picking up the coffee cup left on the table in the waiting area? While this may seem like a small thing, your business reputation is at stake here. The risk of arguing with a neighbor is not good for business, so be clear on these terms from the beginning.

"My colleague to the left was a total slob! He left towels everywhere and would let his color bowls stack up until the end of the day. I had to move stations in the salon, so my customers didn't have to look at it!"

Marcus' neighbor's behavior negatively impacted his business; there was a complete lack of professionalism. The salon where he rented his space had no rules in its lease regarding tidiness and general conduct on-site. Marcus had no choice but to deal with it or break his lease and start over somewhere else.

Of course, you can remedy that particular issue by leasing an enclosed suite. This will minimize the challenges for an immediate neighbor but will not guarantee that your client has an engaging experience getting to your front door.

Toni and Dan's situation was different:

"Our lease clearly spelled out our responsibility for maintaining the area in front of our storefront. We could plant flowers in pots and make the area complement the salon. What we were not clear on was how far from the front door we were responsible for. When the parking area was updated, we received a bill for a portion of the cost."

Dan had overlooked the common area maintenance fees for the entire shopping center, which was a part of their responsibility. Missing this crucial detail impacted two significant parts of his business; operating expenses and profits.

You will want to consider who bears the cost of Common Area Maintenance as well as Real Estate Taxes (RETs). Most building leases will call this information out in the lease; however, a lease station within a building might not be as clear.

Storage: How much space do you need for your supplies and cleaning equipment?

Depending on your state or commonwealth requirements, there are supplies you will need to access beyond color and perms. Consider bleach and other common cleansers; evaluate the necessary venting requirements to ensure your service area is free from fumes. This will be driven by the services you plan to offer.

How often you will order supplies is also driven by the amount of storage space available to you. In the next chapter, we will talk about cash flow, which will also impact your ordering cycles.

Angie commented "I only had one customer who regularly got a perm. The supplier I used had a minimum order of six each time I bought some - that was more than a year's supply. I hated having to store them and probably still have some in the closet!"

For Angie, this meant she was utilizing valuable space in her storage area.

That space has a cost from a rental perspective; Angie was consuming the costly space she was paying for. Not only were the unused perms taking up extra space, they wouldn't soon be used.

When contemplating what space you need, consider how your surrounding environment impacts your day-to-day business, and will you have any control of it?

Another consideration is space for products you may choose to sell. This impacts both your storage space and your service area. Retailing products to customers is a significant revenue stream, so why not? To be successful in product sales, you need them displayed. Customers must be aware that you have the product they want. Display items in a way that creates interest in knowing the product's purpose.

It is crucial to ensure you have a strong visual display, even in a single-chair environment. Customers must have a clear view of the products available. When a unit sells, you need to replenish it as soon as possible; customers may not ask if you have the desired product if they don't see it.

To ensure you aren't running to a nearby closet every time you make a sale, you have to plan storage for back stock. Make the most of your valuable time, keep back stock close by, and know how many units you have on hand. Know the MOQs every time you order; this will ensure you plan enough space. Six units of a hair spray may not sound like a lot of space is needed but think of how many products you plan to sell and multiply that by six. A closet can fill up quickly.

Dirty Laundry: When thinking of space, be clear on your plan for doing laundry on a daily basis. Is there a laundry on-site, or do you plan to take it home and return with your towels and capes the next workday?

On average, each customer will use three towels per visit, assuming your business is balanced between cuts and chemical services. These will stack up quickly; manage the wet towels appropriately. You certainly don't want your room to smell of damp, musty towels.

This applies to chemical robes for your customers as well. Angie shared through frustration, "I thought keeping up with laundry for two kids was a chore. I had no concept that I would be taking six or seven robes' homes every day to be cleaned for the next day's services."

She did not have access to laundry on-site; it added time and effort to every day she worked. She couldn't put it off until the weekend as she had her home responsibilities to manage as well. She didn't want to spend money on enough robes to go an entire week without doing laundry.

The salon Marcus worked in had a laundry room with a washer and dryer in the building. This was convenient, but he constantly fought other stylists to access the units.

"Imagine eight of us trying to do our laundry at the same time. None of us wants to stay late or come in early just to wash towels - it is very frustrating!"

Dan and Toni took the route of having someone on staff who did nothing but keep up laundry and fill/dust retail shelves. While this was an excellent solution for stylists to focus on client services, it cost the business—a labor expense that reduced the salon's profit.

The last part of space to consider is where you will wash your customer's hair.

The Shampoo Bowl.

A no-brainer, right?

Keep in mind that the bowl utilizes floor space and has plumbing connections and pipes.

You are probably thinking - "What's the big deal?"

Two reasons why I think it is important to consider this is:

1. You pay for the amount of space you are renting. If you have a bowl in your room, that's an excellent convenience for you and your client, but it comes with a cost per square foot and services. Your lease payment will include the price for that space and a water consumption charge.

   If shampoo bowls are in a common area, the cost is split across all service providers, reducing the overall cost to renters.

2. When something breaks or clogs, who is responsible for the repair cost? If it's in your room, it will most likely be determined to be your fault. You may have the pleasure of paying the plumber's fee as well.

The reality is you pay for this utility one way or another; your landlord will have passed these costs onto you as part of your rental fee.

It's part of the cost of doing business, whether a single chair or not. You have to decide how the price best suits your business model.

Certificate of Occupancy

Have you ever heard of a CO? In addition to other licenses and permits necessary to operate a business, the space you work from will require a CO from the city or town where you work.

If you are leasing a station in a multi-chair facility, the landlord will bear the burden of obtaining the CO. Ask the questions and make sure a current permit exists. You don't want to show up one day to work and find the main doors bolted shut because the owner didn't renew or maintain the permit.

If you lease space to others, you are most likely responsible for having the proper permits. Getting a CO will vary by jurisdiction, so talk to the appropriate city department and understand the requirements.

Be sure you know all of the licenses required to run your shop. Single chair owners may need a different license in addition to a hairdressing license to work independently. Check with your State Board to clarify what additional licensing you might need.

Along with knowing who is responsible for the common areas, assessing these needs will help you find a suitable space.

On average, a single-chair lease space is around 120 square feet for a personal suite. (The equivalent of a ten by twelve-foot room.) Most likely, this space will include a single shampoo bowl and storage closet.

If you are going the multi-chair salon route, I recommend allowing approximately seventy-two square feet per chair. As of the writing of this book, Covid 19 Pandemic has brought to mind the need for space between us. The plus side is that an open-air salon will feel more spacious; the downside is the cost per square foot.

As with all of it, ensure it is safe and easily controlled. An unlocked closet or counter is an invitation for things to disappear.

Grab a pen and paper and do an estimate to what space you need.

☐ **How much room for storage of back up products and supplies?**

☐ **How many products are you going to retail and how much display space do you need?**

☐ **Where are you going to store your used towels and robes?**

☐ **Are all the Licenses and Permits in place to operate the business?**

CHAPTER 6

MAKING MONEY

So you are off on your new adventure, intending to make lots of money.

What exactly does making money mean?

Let's be real here: Yes, you may be joining the hair dressing ranks because you have a passion for it; but if you aren't intent on making money while enjoying your passion, hard days lie ahead.

Success, Winning, Being on top; all require greenbacks (or these days 'bitcoins') to keep doing what you love.

Being an entrepreneur is more than just opening your door and saying, "Here I am - the greatest stylist in all the world!"

Confidence is necessary for success but it will not put cash in the bank or pay your vendors.

Suppose your sole focus is to dress hair or provide spa services and do nothing more; in that case, you should consider working in a commission-based salon. Let someone else worry about running the business.

No discouragement intended - just stating the obvious. The goal of this book is to guide you toward the success you want. Don't leave the greatest industry around because you are unhappy; figure out the challenges and push forward.

When people talk about making money, they are (whether they know it or not) talking about Revenue. Revenue, in short, is the amount of money that comes into the business. It doesn't matter if it's cash, bitcoin, E-Pay, or credit payment; it all adds up to revenue.

For your CPA, Revenue will have a little different meaning, but for the person without a financial background, we will stick with *all money coming in.*

The next important part of the equation is expenses, everything you spend to operate your business. Expenses will include things such as rent, insurance, supplies, products, taxes, etc. Depending on how your business is structured, one of the expenses may be salaries and/or labor costs. This is very important for your CPA to help you determine: the tax implications for claiming a wage if you are self-employed could be devastating if not reported correctly.

Profit is the more important term, in my opinion.

Why? You ask.

Because profit refers to the money that is yours to keep and spend on whatever you want.

Profit is arrived at by subtracting expenses from revenue. The leftover not obligated to the business is your profit. It is most likely obligated to pay your mortgage and personal expenses, but that is separate from the business. It is imperative that you keep them separate from each other.

I cannot stress enough the importance of a CPA to help you with this. Rules and taxation schedules change often; part of the accountant's job is to keep up with the changes and apply the rules to your business. As an owner of a business (sole proprietor or partnership), you won't have time to read about tax law changes and adequately service your clientele.

The business structure you settled on from the first chapter becomes hugely crucial at this point. Financial reporting quickly becomes an intermeshed set of numbers that move from credits to debits and vice versa; this will cause great strife if you aren't careful.

Let's go back to Revenue.

Each time you receive a payment for a service provided, this payment becomes business income. Even as a self-employed stylist, this money is considered income. I point this out as that money is not discretionary; it has to be tracked within the business.

You don't have to track it but be prepared for the repercussions. The Tax Representative will have no sympathy for your choices.

Regardless of how you receive the payment, it should be logged into a ledger. Numerous apps and software are available to track *sales*.

At the end of the day, I literally mean a 24-hour spin of the clock; you want to know how much revenue you received and the correlation to the services that generated the sale. If every customer had haircuts, this is important to know as your only cost for the service was your time and space. If you performed colors or perms, that's critical to know as an additional cost to the service beyond your time was included.

Are you lost yet? Don't panic; it will all make sense shortly.

"I never worried about tracking what services I did until I went to buy a new car. I couldn't prove what my personal income was because I wasn't tracking expenses."

Angie ran into this issue when her bank asked her to show proof of income. She didn't have 1040s from a company to prove what she earned and brought home. The lender wanted more information to prove she was a viable candidate for a loan.

Marcus, on the other hand (the cheeky one with the S-Corp), had all the business records to verify the business' bottom line and his salary.

Expenses are tricky; understanding how money is organized and categorized is critical. There are key categories you want to know for other business reasons. At the end of the day, they all add up to an expense, but if you aren't aware of how money flows out, you can't plan for the future of your business.

Should the IRS question your expenses, it is not wise to rely on your memory of the payment, much less NOT have a receipt to verify the expense.

Primary expenses to track are:

- Rent

- Insurance

- Salaries (if they exist)

- Advertising

- Supplies

- Entertainment (Be careful with this one)

These are in no particular order. Expenses are grouped into fixed and variable expenses for tax and planning purposes. Fixed expenses are items that don't change from month to month over an extended period of time (usually six or twelve months); variable expenses change each payment cycle depending on demand. Each of these will most likely have sub-categories that fit your type of business.

Ohhhh - and I forgot Taxes. Those don't just come due at the end of the year as mentioned previously. Remember Angie?

Your categories and tracking of these outflows will help you understand how your business spends money. Should the profit be lean, it's easy to assess what categories are consuming the revenue.

"At the end of the year, Dan looked at how much we spent on Entertainment expenses for our customers. We quickly figured out we had to cut back on the cost of the wine we provided as it was impacting the profit." - Toni.

You may encounter expenses that are one-time fees or only occur once a year; these can be lumped into the *other* category. It's a balancing act to ensure you track enough categories to answer business questions while not generating *data death*.

I mentioned being careful with entertainment expenses. The government is very clear about this write-off. As of this writing, only 50% of your entertainment expenses can be written off. This can change depending on what Congress enacts, so check with your CPA to stay up to date.

Marcus took vacations with his clients to write off the trip as a business expense. He intended to have a lavish trip and reduce his S-Corp tax payments.

"It was great every year when I took elaborate vacations, I wrote them off as business expenses. I like all my clients; I didn't mind traveling with them so I could call it entertainment."

Entertainment expenses are a write-off for money spent on the customer, all personal expenses are devalued under IRS rules.

When he was audited, he was penalized for this. He was only entitled to a reduction of half of his expenses and none of his husband's expenses. It became a more significant issue when it was determined that he was staying as a guest at his client's condo on the Riviera. He had no expense for lodging and was technically receiving payment in kind for services rendered. Marcus was being a Wobbler. Once again his lack of information to his book keeper was going to cost him in the long run.

I don't know about you, but a vacation to me is meant to be away from customers and find time to recharge my batteries. I don't think traveling on a tax credit is worth the effort.

All these lead up to profit and how it is determined. All things said, it is simply calculation:

Revenue

-

Expenses

=

Profit

Example:

June Sales Income $1,000

June Expenses - $750

June Profit = $250

It is more technical than this, and that is why you hire a good CPA. They will drill down into how your offset accounts are managed.

A crucial part of being profitable is managing your Cash Flow. Cash Flow, in short, is a snapshot of money in and money out. How does it ebb and flow?

For the salon business, cash flow is relatively simple. You receive payment from your clients for the services rendered, and you pay your bills. Right?

Not exactly.

In order to perform your services, you need a place to work. Chances are you paid your rent a month in advance. So you spent money before you had any coming in.

You need color, peroxide, perms, towels, and shampoo before you can meet your client's request.

So how does that work?

This is where cash flow comes in. You have to be able to pay for your necessary supplies and location before working, most likely by using a credit card, which is due in 30 days. Now you have a financial obligation against future income.

When you receive payment for the service, a part of that cash belongs to the credit card company. Your projected expenses should be tracked so you don't spend more than you can pay.

Let's go back to that example from June. At the end of the month, we had $250.00 in profit. What happens if I have $300 due on my credit card in July?

Do I take the $250 and enjoy a charming evening out on the town, or do I hold it back to apply toward the credit card bill coming due?

The money for the credit card payment is outlined in the expense column and should be set aside to pay the bill when it is due.

In theory, yes you can spend that $250 on a wonderful evening out if you have looked at your projected expenses.

Am I wholly booked for next month, and am I sure I will meet my expected income of $1,000? Do my predicted expenses add up to more than $1,000?

I think you understand where I am going with this; if you have money coming in and it's more than what's going out, you are probably safe to spend some of that profit. But proceed with caution - a solid practice for any business is to have six months of averaged profits saved for a rainy day.

What is predictive income?

In order to assess what income you will have over the next earnings period, you will need to calculate how much money you expect to make.

A good practice is to understand what your earning potential is. How does one do that?

Look at your business model and determine how many services you can perform daily. This is all contingent on the service mix. We can't predict the future, but we can hypothesize the outcome.

Let's say you are focused on nothing but haircuts and blowouts. For an 8-hour day, each service being 45 minutes, you have the potential to perform ten services per an eight hour day (this includes time for a nourishment and a bathroom break).

Assuming you charge $50 for a cut and style, your earning potential is $500 daily. Then multiply by how many days you plan to work, say four days a week.

4 X 500 = $2,000

List the services you plan to offer and make up a pretend map of the perfect schedule; two highlights and cuts, three blowouts, and four haircuts. Whatever the day might look like for you. Remember - we are only estimating here.

Start Time	Time Blocks
10:00 AM	15m

My Perfect Schedule

TIME	SUNDAY	MONDAY	TUESDAY	WEDNESDAY	THURSDAY	FRIDAY	SATURDAY
10:00 AM			Haircut/Blow				
10:15 AM			$50.00				
10:30 AM							
10:45 AM			Highlight				
11:00 AM			$125.00				
11:15 AM							
11:30 AM			Haircut				
11:45 AM			$35				
12:00 PM			Haircut/Blow				
12:15 PM			$50.00				
12:30 PM							
12:45 PM			Lunch				
1:00 PM							
1:15 PM			Color				
1:30 PM			$80.00				
1:45 PM			Haircut/Blow				
2:00 PM			$50.00				
2:15 PM							
2:30 PM			Haircut/Blow				
2:45 PM			$50.00				
3:00 PM							
3:15 PM			Highlight				
3:30 PM			$125.00				
3:45 PM							
4:00 PM			Haircut/Blow				
4:15 PM			$50.00				
4:30 PM							
4:45 PM			Haircut/Blow				
5:00 PM			$50.00				
5:15 PM							
5:30 PM			Color				
5:45 PM			$80.00				
6:00 PM			Haircut				
6:15 PM			$35				
6:30 PM			Haircut/Blow				
6:45 PM			$50.00				
7:00 PM							

Include essential information with each service.

How much do you plan to charge for a service?

How much time are you going to spend on each service?

This may seem overwhelming - don't let it consume you.

First step is to create a list of services and fees; you need that information for your customers anyway.

On a side note: Please don't make the mistake of charging different fees to different customers. That's a great way to lose business when someone finds out a friend is paying less than they are. Be very clear on your pricing structure. Be fair and know your value in the marketplace.

Secondly, compile information for what you will spend on rent and supplies.

Take the amount you expect to generate weekly and reduce that by 20%. The reality is that clients get sick and/or cancel. Maybe they forgot their appointment time or showed up late and had to reschedule. The point is that interruptions will occur that reduce the perfect day. If there are no exceptions - you are ahead of the game, but when planning, use caution.

With your weekly revenue determined, estimate your expenses. How much supply debt is required to perform those highlights? What is the rent and insurance cost per week?

Here's an example:

$790	Revenue
-$38	Cost of Chemicals
-$33	Misc. EXP
-$100	Day's Rent
$619	Profit

By adding up the potential services: Revenue = $790.00. I used $38.00 worth of color and bleach to perform the services. If I add in my rent for the day of $100.00 plus miscellaneous costs of $33.00, I project I will generate a profit of $619.00 that day.

So, I can predict to make $619 a day; if I work four days a week, that's $2476 a week! How Exciting! Don't forget to calculate that 20% loss we discussed. Now, we are at $1980 a week. Not a bad rate of pay.

Be consistent with your schedule. Flexibility is good to a point, but be wary of time variations and how the changes might impact your personal life. Whether an individual or a multi-chair salon, take the time to play out this scenario. Solidifying how your profits look long term will positively influence your decisions.

What you are looking to determine is how much profit you can expect week after week.

Spending the time to estimate your earnings potential and profit will guide you toward building a solid business. This exercise will drive flaws in the business model to the surface. Perhaps your service fees don't support the suite you want to lease. Does the color price capture the cost of supplies and your time and space?

Consider how to sustain your personal expenses if your business life is impacted. Could you produce a living should the business model suddenly change?

Understanding your revenue stream and your expenses, you can easily determine how profitable your business is and what it can be long term.

Making money?

☐ **Revenue means what?**

☐ **What are expenses?**

☐ **How do I calculate my profit**

☐ **Why do I need Cash Flow?**

☐ **Should I estimate my income?**

CHAPTER 7

TAXATION

This chapter is dedicated to our favorite subject which no one likes: Taxes.

Taxes occur in many forms:

- ❖ Income

- ❖ Social Security

- ❖ Medicare

- ❖ Sales

- ❖ Franchise

Depending on your business's location, additional taxes may be levied against you.

Real Estate and Property Taxes also exist, but you are paying those with your rent payment to the landlord more than likely.

If you have ever filed a tax return, you know the income tax imposed against you is based on your income; this is still true as a business owner. However, your business structure will determine the taxation scheme. This simply means whether you will pay corporate and/or personal income taxes.

One common misunderstanding in personal income tax is the percentage paid. It is a complicated formula. It isn't as simple as saying I am in the X tax bracket. Do your homework and rely on your resources to plan for the payments.

Taxes are generally prepaid quarterly to the IRS; the amount is determined on an income estimate. What amount is due at the end of the year? When you are starting up, this is probably challenging to figure out. Use the formula for predicting your personal income from the previous chapter to help estimate your tax liability.

Suppose you have set up the business as a corporation and are taking a salary from the company. In that case, the business will pay estimated taxes as scheduled; salary taxes are withheld and communicated through the payroll report and year-end tax form.

This rule applies across all salaries within the business. If you have multiple employees and are withholding their taxes (as you should be), I highly recommend keeping a separate banking account to ensure you have that money set aside.

In addition to Angie being unaware of the need to file and pay quarterly taxes; she also didn't know the requirements of Social Security and Medicare.

"I remember being told by a previous employer that the Social Security fee was 7.25% of my income. I had diligently put this money away every month to cover the expense and was hugely surprised when I found out it was twice that amount."

Angie failed because she didn't understand that her previous employer had paid half of the Social Security payment. As an employer, the business carries responsibility for a portion of the social security liability.

This means that a self-employed individual pays the entire tax amount. If you set up a Corporation or Partnership, the total amount is still due; it is just divided up and reported differently.

Dan didn't take a salary from the business; all income was reported on Toni's salary. With multiple chairs in the salon, they planned for and paid their taxes quarterly as required.

The challenge was, "Putting aside money for prepaying taxes was a serious impact on our cash flow. We didn't allocate our overheads correctly initially, and when the tax payments were due, we had to borrow money."

The issue for them; they didn't plan accordingly for taxes on the employees' social security, which reduced their cash on hand when the quarterly taxes had to be filed. They encountered some additional issues relating to filing requirements. Once they hired a CPA to explain what they needed to do in the future, the issue was easily remedied. It didn't fix the cash flow issue; they had to adjust other business strategies as well.

This is an excellent example of utilizing your resources. Dan was a successful businessman and assumed he understood it all - reality was that he should have sought help from his resources, and he could have avoided the hiccup in the business.

Medicare is another tax that exists, and you pay for it, just like social security—nothing special to say on that except plan for it.

Sales Tax varies from state to state and is impacted by local jurisdiction requirements. You can easily find out the local tax rate and most likely already know the percentage without realizing it.

You must know the tax requirements in the locality of your business. Generally speaking, products sold are always taxed (your business is considered the retailer, which implies you purchased from a wholesaler leaving the tax liability on you). Services may or may not be taxed. Again, determine this by checking your local government requirements.

Know what they are. If you don't charge your customer's sales tax as your local governance dictates, you will bear the responsibility.

Be In The Know On This Subject!

If your state audits you and determines you didn't file or pay your sales tax as required, they may take legal action and revoke your sales permit or place a lien against your business. Please remember to apply for your sales tax permit before your start selling products.

Last on my list is the Franchise tax. You are probably wondering why I bring this up. You are setting up an independent business and are not part of a Franchise. In this case, the term franchise is a tax term. It is not related to becoming a part of an organization as a Franchisee. This tax varies by state and will determine how you set up the business.

It's generally a relatively small percentage every year, but it is a liability that has to be paid - so be prepared for it.

"As a stylist, I knew my services didn't get taxed for sales. My CPA warned me to make sure and charge taxes for any product I sold. I decided to include the tax in the sales price to make it easier, but the way I set it up in my sales app wasn't right, and I wound up paying extra tax at the end of the year."

What Marcus did was not uncommon; he included the tax cost in the product's sale price. Where he made a mistake was listing the sale price in his accounting software with the tax included. His CPA couldn't quickly discern the actual profit or tax liability. In addition to being taxed at the higher product value, Marcus paid his accountant extra money to determine the issue and fix it moving forward.

In Chapter 6, I spoke about cash flow and estimated liabilities. Taxes will most likely be the most significant impact on both of these categories.

So that you know - the tax authorities are very astute. They have probably witnessed every attempt imaginable to get around paying the taxes due. If you choose to take them on, be prepared for a battle not easily won when you get caught.

Before we stop discussing Taxes, let's go back to Marcus, The Cheeky One. Marcus was attempting to do the right thing by keeping up with his taxes and tracking his income revenue - for the most part.

One day a customer paid him cash. The idea popped into his head; he didn't need to claim the payment. He didn't post the payment to his accounting app. No big deal - the IRS wouldn't miss this small amount. Seeing the benefit of not paying the income tax appealed to him, and he began urging his customers to pay via e-pay for services.

Because he incorrectly reported the social security taxes, the business was flagged by the IRS to set up an audit. When the IRS reviewed his service log, he was in the hot seat to explain all the services scheduled he didn't get paid for.

He claimed they were either no-shows or cancellations, appointments he forgot to remove from his schedule. That sounds like a good reason, right? The IRS agent tracked the e-payments to Marcus' banking account and found a pattern of *no-shows* to e-payments.

"I was stupid to try and cheat the IRS. First off - I am not really that kind of person, but I got greedy. I mean, who doesn't hate how much money goes to the government? I was lucky - I could have gone to jail and ruined my career trying to make a few extra bucks!"

Marcus was fortunate; he got off with a penalty fee. He had to pay interest on the back taxes as well. Trying to cheat the government will haunt you because you will always be looking over your shoulder.

I am of the opinion; your integrity is far more important than a few dollars in the bank. At the end of the day, why would you trade your freedom for a few dollars?

☐ What is the best way to avoid penalties and late filing fees?

A ___ ___ ___ .

CHAPTER 8

SUPPLIES

Initially, it may appear unnecessary to commit an entire chapter to supplies. I mean, seriously, you buy what you need to service your clients, and that is that.

Supplying your business involves many more factors than you may realize, which is why we will look at it.

Think back to Chapter 6 and the importance of tracking expenses. All your supplies and everything you purchase to run your business are considered a material necessity; these are expenses.

The nice Hikari scissors you paid $1,500 for, the full-sleeved cape to keep the hair off your clients, and the color swatch books are all an expense and considered supplies, just as your chemicals are. They all fall under the cost of doing business. (You may hear the term COGS, an acronym for the Cost Of Goods and Supplies.)

A significant part of your supply expense will be chemicals. You will need color, developer, and perms; these items should be readily available to you at a moment's notice.

To effectively do this, you must establish the brands you want to represent your work and determine how you will purchase and manage your stock. There are several great companies out there with varying services to help you stay focused on your clientele and not spend time focused on supplies.

Along with support services, there will be additional costs incurred. If you want weekly delivery, the price per unit will be higher than a vendor where you pick up the product.

How much of your time, not spent dressing hair, do you want to spend picking up stock?

Another consideration is how much money you must spend to earn freebies.

Most companies offer tiered service levels, and with those levels, you can expect support. For example, if you only purchase ten tubes of color per month, you will most likely have to buy your swatch book.

At 1,200 tubes per month, a swatch book is most likely included.

These are just examples you might want to explore.

How will your business partners (I.e., Suppliers) support your business?

At the end of the day, regardless of the supplier's size, you are their customer. Never let a business, even though they might be well known, treat you like they are doing you a favor for letting you use their products. You are paying them and ultimately supporting their business.

We talked earlier about storage in your space. Do you have room to buy products once a month, or do you need weekly deliveries?

Order frequency and turn time are critical factors you need to know about your supplies.

How often you order is driven by space; how long an item stays in the storage closet is defined as Turn Time. Turns are tricky initially but will become less of a challenge as your business develops.

Remember Angie with her one client who got a perm? The turn time on the six perms she had to buy was 18 months, meaning she wouldn't have to repurchase perms for a year and a half. Knowing she was out the expense of the perms due to the minimum buy; she might have considered running to the beauty supply a week or two before her client came in for her perm. If the client changes her style and gives up perming, Angie now has a two or three-year supply that will most likely expire before getting used.

Be aware of industry trends and manage your stock levels accordingly. If you are in a highly conservative area where most everyone is highlighted, keep lighteners on hand and maybe one tube of green for that trendy customer who stops in.

If you have to throw materials away because they have expired, keep track of them. It is a loss to the business and should be captured in the expense column.

All of this is an impact on cash flow. If you buy a month's worth of product at a time, you should receive a better price than buying weekly; this equates to more cash flow out but improves your profit because your materials cost less.

Perhaps you are fortunate enough to work in a strip mall with a beauty supply store nearby. If you plan to go and buy products whenever you need them, you need to analyze this practice. Is this good customer service, and how does the material cost impact your business? There is certainly an argument to be had: on-demand purchases minimize cash flow but reduce profits. The increased cost of materials for the service impacts the bottom line.

On-demand VS pay later: How does it impact your profitability?

Take into consideration the time maintaining supplies; whether the materials are delivered to you, or you run to the beauty supply to get them, this is non-valued work time. The cost here is time spent on an activity that doesn't produce income. Look back to Chapter 6, the part where you estimated what your business revenue would be based on active work time. We planned for eight-hour workdays with lunch; that seems fair enough. But when do you order supplies or wash your laundry?

This is time spent working but not generating any income. It's part of the business, and you have to do it. Suddenly, your 32-hour work week just became a 40-hour work week, and your hourly rate per hour just dropped 20 percent.

This non-valued work cost should play into your decision about how you partner with your vendors; your time spent being productive behind the chair by letting your supplier deliver your products may well justify the extra cost for the materials.

How will vendor perks help you generate more income during work hours? Think about what kind of perks you are getting from your suppliers.

Perks can include freebies, as I mentioned earlier. Perhaps it is a swatch board or maybe an early payment discount. Assess these perks and how they will benefit your business.

In setting up your business relationship, the supplier is going to establish the terms of the relationship. This is driven by how much you buy, your personal/ business credit score, and the length of time you have purchased from them.

Terms for small businesses are usually credit card payment upon order. Convenient for both parties, but know that you are paying a premium for this convenience. Suppliers pay transaction fees for processing those credit cards (just like you will for processing how you get paid). Those fees are added to the total cost of the material. Some vendors will show the fee as a line item; some just build it into their price.

Not all suppliers will offer a discount for early payments or cash, but it is worth asking and comparing other companies' practices. A one percent savings might not seem like a lot, but it does add up, and why not take advantage of improving your bottom line any way you legally can? This is your opportunity to ask your supplier what discount you can expect if you pay with cash or check.

If they don't accept cash-like payments or offer discounts, ask about setting up payment terms. How this generally works is that you receive your products along with an invoice. On that invoice will be a note of when payment is due. It might be 30 days (if you have excellent credit and are buying at volumes high enough to warrant the time); it might say due on receipt. When setting up payment terms, always request an early payment discount. If the invoice is due in 30 days, can you expect to receive a discount on the invoice total? (This would apply to products purchased - not to shipping and handling fees.)

My experience has been that after a year of paying by credit card, the vendor might be willing to move you to Net terms. This is important as it will likely save you on fees and will help with your cash flow. Be mindful that they will not willingly offer you perks; you must ask for them! And don't be shy about asking for a discount.

Do you know your salesperson? Have you met with the person who is being paid to support you?

Every supplier out there offers some form of support. It is imperative that you know whom to call when you have an issue. What's the direct line to customer care if your order was incorrect? The best path, in my mind, is by calling your sales rep. Their income is directly related to your being satisfied and buying more products. A good salesperson will want to have a relationship with you and welcome the opportunity to resolve an issue. If they don't, I suggest you let their superior know; if that doesn't resolve the issue, move on to a company that will support you appropriately.

Delivery fees are another area you want to understand the cost. Know the shipping and handling cost and ask for it to be itemized on the invoice. Some companies prefer to lump their fees into one total, masking hidden profit centers for their business. Yes, we are all in business to make money, but zealous business people know where they spend their money. If they don't itemize the cost, ask that the products ship on your account number. Setting up your own delivery account is a great way to control costs and know where that money is going. Any of the three major carriers welcome small business relationships. One caveat to remember is that a large supplier has probably negotiated highly discounted shipping rates, which might be less expensive. If they are masking handling fees, you won't know but can compare their shipping rate to your independent rate and determine which one is best for your business. In the end, know the impact on your business.

In a single-chair situation, the savings opportunities will be less than in a multi-chair salon. It might be worthwhile to find out what products your colleagues are using and perhaps place purchase orders together to earn some of the perks available.

Think of ways to create a Co-Op that allows several service providers to join forces and save some money.

If you are doing all the work to support the Co-Op, don't be shy about taking a percentage for your time and effort. Just make sure you tell your co-op members your plan so they don't feel cheated.

Finally, I want to tie supply costs to your long-term business model and their impact on Taxes from Chapter 7.

Certain items are considered fixed assets and have a different impact on how they are tracked. This is driven by the item's value and how it might be depreciated.

If you are leasing a suite or chair in a salon, the likelihood of owning any fixed assets is improbable. That said, make sure to track any expense you have for your business so your accountant can determine depreciation over time.

For example, the sheers you paid $1,500 for might depreciate over five years. That translates to a deduction against your revenue for the next five years. Why would that be important? It's a business strategy that suggests you will make more money next year and need more expenses to reduce your tax liability. Depreciating assets is one way to accomplish this.

Most tax software, or your accountant, will advise when it's appropriate to list an expense as an asset with long-term depreciation.

Asset terminology is daunting: in laypeople's terms, an asset is anything that has value and can be sold to raise cash. Lease stations generally have few assets, whereas a full-service salon will have many.

For a multi-chair salon, fixed assets with depreciation schedules are much more straightforward; the station and chair, chemical processors, etc.

What to watch for:

☐ **Order frequency**

☐ **Turn Time**

☐ **Discounts**

☐ **Support**

☐ **Fees**

CHAPTER 9

INSURANCE

Insurance in the salon industry is not generally a topic given much attention. I think it needs some attention in the lawsuit-happy world we live in.

Anytime you own a business, you are at risk of being sued. Whether it is an unhappy customer with brassy highlights or someone who slipped on a wet floor and broke her hip, there is a risk of being sued.

It is easy to say, "I don't really have anything, so what are they going to get?"

That's a childish evasion of a serious matter. As a business owner, you should do all you can to protect yourself against unforeseen events and losses.

How you protect yourself is dependent on which business structure you choose.

As a business owner, your personal assets may be on the table should you get sued. Consider any equity you have in your home or cars, retirement accounts, bonds, and stocks; any item in your name with a positive cash value can be attacked.

What I am addressing here is liability insurance. In order to protect your assets, you want to look at carrying professional liability insurance. Regardless of whether a client is hurt or is just pissed off at you, having insurance will provide some level of protection.

There are still other issues, such as legal fees, court costs, etc., but at least this will help you keep your assets.

Multiple companies exist to provide this type of coverage, but I recommend speaking with your personal insurance carrier for recommendations; if they don't offer some kind of coverage, they should know who might help you.

You may feel that all your clients love you and would never sue you; get a quote, and decide if the risk of not having it available is worth it.

We all think our residence won't burn down, but most US homeowners pay for insurance just in case. Think about how you plan to protect your business long-term.

Along that thought line, be mindful to avoid opportunities to get sued. Keep your area clean, and be on the lookout for water spills or slippery surfaces. A moment of cleanup could save you a lot of hassle and money down the road.

One option to help protect your personal assets is to set up your business as an LLC. This does not stop the opportunity of your business from being sued, but it does shift where the responsibility lies. Now, if you are negligent or are manipulating how money flows in and out of your business, an LLC is not bulletproof.

The rules and protections for the LLC structure vary state by state; your lawyer can best advise you on how to complete this model.

A sole proprietor can be an independent LLC in some cases; the implication is you must appropriately manage the financial aspects of the business. Separate business and personal accounts are critical. If you blur the lines, the opportunity to have the courts treat business and personal now becomes one.

For multiple chair salons, the business owners should manage professional liability insurance on the company.

If you are leasing your chair or suite, ask the owner where their liabilities end. With that information, and the assistance of legal counsel and an insurance provider's guidance, you can determine what is appropriate for your business.

Let's look at what happened to Marcus:

"My client fell, walking to my station. Someone spilled water on the floor, sending her down to the concrete within a second. She sued the salon owner, and me, for negligence."

Marcus' salon leased the stations to each stylist, and they had coverage for the business, but it didn't flow down to the stylist. And as you will recall, Marcus was set up as an S-Corp, and he carried no professional liability insurance coverage.

"I thought my career was over; there was no way I could have paid for her medical and legal costs."

Marcus was lucky; the suit settled out of court. It was determined the salon carried the responsibility after the customer stated Marcus was walking behind her. He was not negligent as he could not have seen the water and thereby could not have prevented the accident. Marcus now carries professional liability insurance.

Dan and Toni had a little different situation:

"A car drove through the front of our salon. Luckily no one was seriously injured, but several people got cut by the flying glass. One customer sued us, along with the individual driving the car."

For Dan and Toni, there was no liability as this was beyond their control. They had insurance to cover the suit if it progressed; the impact to them was the legal fees to show the driver to be negligent.

The other part to consider is Personal Property Insurance. If you are leasing a chair or suite, who has the responsibility should something happen to your personal items? All those expenses for supplies and service items get destroyed in a fire? Who has to pay to replace them?

Imagine those Hikari sheers taking a walk from your station while you were at the shampoo bowl washing out your client's color.

How do you recover that cost?

This type of insurance is generally referred to as contents insurance.

It is highly doubtful that a lease station or suite would carry contents insurance on your personal items. Ask the question, just to be sure.

As a full-service salon with commission employees, offering some level of content insurance for your team is a great benefit, but payouts can be a nightmare if you don't manage it upfront. Just like taking photos of your home items, producing a list of items in your *shop* and their value is a prudent step to take. Just imagine your salon burns down; you commit to replacing curling irons and sheers, and to your surprise, all your stylists recently acquired high-end German sheers.

Like taxes, insurance expenses can be annoying until you realize you need it and didn't get it.

What are the two common types of insurance a salon owner should have?

1.

2.

CHAPTER 10

EDUCATION

If you have recently finished school and received your license - Congratulations!

You are entering into an exciting career field with limitless opportunities. As you explore the multitude of options, you will experience amazing people and tons of creativity.

You may think that you learned everything you need to know in school, but the reality is that there is still much to learn. Armed with strong basic skills, the next level of excellence is up to you.

How do you get there?

Education.

Even seasoned stylists should continue their education as styles and trends constantly evolve in the Arts and Sciences of dressing hair.

As a salon owner, you may think this is not important. You have all the other aspects of the business you need to manage; spending time on education seems unnecessary.

I will argue that point with you: if you stop learning and developing, you will become stagnant, and your business will suffer.

Should you operate in a state that requires Continuing Education to renew your license, keep in mind that CEs are not enough. While they generally remind you of the basics of acceptable salon practices, they rarely update you on new trends.

Another critical benefit to educating yourself is the opportunity to network within the industry. Working with colleagues to hone your skills, you may meet someone who needs help with their beauty brand. Perhaps they are an influencer and may be able to help you promote your abilities.

Also, think about how you will utilize Social Media to build your client base. If you are not proficient and ahead of the new trends, you will be highly unlikely to impress anyone enough to visit your chair.

If you have employees, set out a plan for them to achieve success through education. When hiring, ensure they understand the need to further their skills and what you, as a leader, are willing to do to help them.

Where do you get this extra knowledge?

Talk to your suppliers about what education they offer to support the use of their products. Many of the more prominent brands provide online training for new product offerings. Think back to your supplier research list; education should be one of the criteria you require before committing to a vendor.

Search the internet for trends and what others are doing. Watch videos for inspiration, and don't be afraid to ask someone to be a model for you to try the concept on.

Will you be 100% successful each time? Not likely! But as I said early in the book - If you aren't willing to try new things, you will never fail and, therefore, never succeed.

Subscribe to trade magazines for inspiration; look to one of the key fashion publications to know what forward fashion is in Europe. Paris is still the go-to for high fashion - know the trends. The trends may not be appropriate for all your clients, but what a renewal of energy you will have with that one client asks for a double Chignon.

First off, you can pat yourself on the back for knowing what it is and how to achieve it. Secondly, think of all the people who will see this unique style and want to know where your client had their hair done.

Don't be afraid to experiment on your own. Chances are you joined this field to be creative, so be creative.

When you have unproductive time behind the chair - don't run to the coffee shop for a latte and watch the latest cat videos! Sure get the latte but spend the time reviewing the latest trends in fashion.

What does all this have to do with owning a salon?

Whether leasing a chair or running a shop with several stylists, keeping up to date on the industry is critical for success.

Single chair owners are less likely to stay abreast of new trends due to the requirements of running their business. This will result in a lack of building your business to the next level. It's a commitment to be your own boss, and this is just one of the elements.

I have continuously talked about having a lawyer and CPA available to you. When you think of their obligation to support you, consider if you would pay for services from an accountant who hasn't read the latest tax laws. Should you be sued, would you expect your attorney to be up to speed on the most recent tort case that might save you? Of course, you would.

So why shouldn't your customers expect you to stay abreast of trends and techniques?

Remember, your customers pay you to make them feel and look beautiful.

List key places you may find the latest trends?

☐

_____

☐

_____

☐

_____

CHAPTER 11

ET-AL

And everything else you need to know.

We have hit the highlights of opening a salon business, be it all on your own or with a partner.

Lots of things to think about; hopefully, you now have a basic sense of business concepts.

Information you weren't aware of before now. As I said, you didn't need to read this if you have an MBA.

That said, I will tell you not to worry if you don't have a college degree. Anyone is capable of owning and running a business. Education is a step up but doesn't guarantee success.

Hard work and persistence do.

Many other requirements are necessary to run your business, and as the world changes every day, more will come to you.

We didn't touch on Social Media; it's essential to your advertising and the growth of the business. While this is critical to your business exposure, exercise caution on the web. I highly recommend that you be mindful. Remember, once you put it out there, you can't take it back. I suggest you manage a personal social media profile and a professional one.

While some of your clients may be friends you socialize with, other customers may not want to see you slamming back tequila shots at the local pub.

Keep your personal life minimally involved in your business life.

A considerable part of my success within the salon and the business world came from my understanding of the power of listening.

My customer's time with me was about them, not about me.

A mentor taught me that lesson early on in my career as a stylist; I carried it into pharmaceutical sales. What it did for me was help me understand what the customer wanted and needed.

Frequently, a customer's time in my chair was about them getting away from their life and talking about something they couldn't discuss with close family or friends; let them vent. It's not your job to be right or grandstand your political views with your customers - it's your job to serve them. That is why they are paying you.

Yes, it is great to be around like-minded people. But be careful about how small you keep your circle; you don't know what you might miss out on.

I am going to quote my brother-in-law, a retired Air Force Colonel,

"You can't hate people you know. Take a moment to listen and learn. It doesn't change who you are but gives you perspective."

Apply that principle to your life as well as your business, and you will find diversity far more significant than you would have ever imagined.

Good Luck

I wish you the best in your new adventure. The Salon and Spa industry is a fantastic world. I am genuinely grateful for the years spent meeting the people who make it thrive.

The last piece of advice I will give you is to seek out a mentor.

Find a seasoned professional within the industry to help guide you. Oftentimes, you already know the answer and just need a sounding board to confirm your direction. Sometimes you will be horribly wrong and need to hear what you don't want to hear.

A significant other may seem like the perfect sounding board, but I caution you; don't make work 100% of your life.

When you are working, work hard, and do your best.

When you are with loved ones, love them, and leave the salon at the salon.

I have a rule at home; work-related issues get ten minutes at the kitchen counter daily, nothing more and hopefully less. A limited time was established to ensure work-life didn't take over love life. Sometimes you need to vent and get things off your chest, but unless your go-to person is a professional in your field or a licensed psychologist, they don't have the necessary skill sets to solve the challenge.

Be mindful not to burden your relationship with what others are doing - make your personal life the focus of what you are doing.

Most importantly, I say to you - Have fun and don't take yourself too seriously!

At the beginning of the book, I identified the personality traits of the hairdressers/owners I interviewed.

The Wobbler, Being Cheeky, and Inquisitive.

Knowing what you have learned from the book, which would you like to be in life and as a business person? Think about each of them.

For me, my life has been a mixture of all three types.

In the salon and spa industry, it is imperative that you be Inquisitive. You must look around you and ask all the questions you don't know the answer to. This is how you will grow both as a stylist and as a business person.

Being Cheeky can be great fun while bringing a specific personality to you and your business. Just be mindful of which lines are OK to cross and which ones are going to get you into serious trouble. It can be fun to be playful and amusing. Sometimes being brash is necessary; I will implore you just always to make sure you are maintaining your integrity.

A favorite quote from a movie is, "A man's integrity is his destiny." Think about what that means to you and apply it to your life.

And being a Wobbler has its value. This allows you to be flexible and fluid in life. Nothing is set in stone, and life will bring you challenges you could have never foreseen. So, maintain an ability to move left or right as needed.

As you are now aware, each and every choice you make as a business owner somehow impacts another part of the business. Owning your own business can provide well for you and your family, but it does come with costs. Be mindful and never assume you know it all and you will do very well in the industry I think of as the Arts and Sciences of Hairdressing.

About the Author

Thadeus Parkland began his hairdressing career in the Dallas/Fort Worth area of Texas. Starting as an apprentice, his fifteen-year tenure with the same company led him to leadership roles in key business areas. Co-managing multiple salons, managing the inventory and supply cycle, and eventually overseeing the business as a whole. The salon owners were amazing mentors to him and provided a strong understanding of how the business operated, both from a human asset and a material perspective. An opportunity to lead a product development project for the company opened the door to moving into the industry's development and manufacturing side.

Working with key industry leaders, the perspective he garnered, along with the knowledge of the manufacturing industry, led him to move into the pharmaceutical industry.

A willingness to learn and create opportunities opened doors and provided successes, one of which was the privilege of retiring from corporate America at fifty-five.

Always connected to his love for the Arts and Sciences of Hairdressing, he was compelled to return to the industry with hopes of helping others achieve their success through consulting.

He began case studies with industry professionals researching the shift in the industry from commission-based salons to independent ownership. What he learned about their challenges is laid out in *10 Things You Should Know*.

If you want more information or would like information on speaking engagements or consulting services, contact him via his publisher, P1Press.

Other works available at P1Press:

8 Things You Should Know To Launch A Product Line

Deathbed Confession: My Son Was A Stolen Baby

The Girl Who Stole My Chair

My Life Being A Sensitive

P1Press

ISBN 979-8-9861673-0-5

9 798986 167305

THE
BUSINESS OWNER'S
FREEDOM
FLYWHEEL

MAKE YOUR BUSINESS
FUN TO **RUN** (NOW)
AND **EASY** TO **SELL** (LATER)

DAWN BLOOMER

SPECIAL INVITATION

Be sure to get all of the bonuses
included in this book.

You'll find them at:

ProductivePressure.com/Flywheel

*To my dad—who always had the best advice,
whether I was ready to hear it or not.*

*When you retired, you said,
"I have enough money
to do everything I ever wanted…
I'm just not sure I have enough time left."*

*I love you for teaching me
how to think, lead, and live.*

*This book is for business owners who want to build
something great without missing out along the
way—who want freedom now, not just someday.*

Notes.

HOW TO USE THIS BOOKMARK:

1. JOT DOWN IDEAS.

2. NOTE WHAT YOU'D LIKE TO WORK ON WITH YOUR COACH.

3. CAPTURE ACTION ITEMS THAT NEED YOUR ATTENTION!

THANKS FOR READING!

TABLE OF CONTENTS

INTRODUCTION

Entrepreneurs are wired differently.

We wear overcommitment like a badge of honor. We're addicted to solving problems, chasing growth, and proving we can do more—*because we can.*

We thrive on the challenge, the hustle, and the satisfaction of making it work. But what happens when the very qualities that drive us forward also start to hold us back?

Many entrepreneurs have been there. They start their journey with a grand vision and unlimited energy. But then the excitement fades and they wind up feeling worn out instead of inspired.

I was no different.

As a veterinarian for racehorses, my truck was my office, my pharmacy, and sometimes even my bedroom. I worked six to seven days a week, was on call 24/7, and I *loved* it.

The drive. The responsibility. The process of figuring everything out. It was *fun*.

When I became a mom, I was determined to prove I could handle it all: the demanding career, the business with its constant demands, and parenting. My newborn son, Jack, spent his days either in the truck with me and our nanny or in a makeshift nursery I'd set up in a tack room in one of the barns. At the time, I thought it was a pretty clever solution—a way to keep him close without sacrificing my clients' needs or my business goals.

Running a business and working full time as a veterinarian wasn't easy. My clients counted on me for everything—calling at all hours with emergencies or questions they didn't trust anyone else with.

My team looked to me to solve problems and give them support. But no matter how much I did, I always felt like I was dropping the ball on something.

I didn't want to miss a moment with Jack, either, but that meant toting him around everywhere. Balancing work and motherhood felt like juggling flaming torches while riding a unicycle.

By the time my daughter, Emma, came along, I took it a step further. I bought an RV, parked it at the racetrack, and made it their home away from home. It gave the kids—and the nanny—more space, a bathroom, and some of the comforts of home.

They were still close to me while I worked. But it also created some additional effort because it meant stocking diapers, bottles, clothes, and supplies in the truck, the RV, and the barn nursery.

I kept telling myself, *These are first-world problems, right? Just make it work.*

And I *did*. Until I couldn't.

One day, I found myself hiding in a too-small barn bathroom stall with my knees pressed against the door, desperate for just five minutes to think.

People were always banging on my truck window, opening the door to ask me a question while I was trying to cram some food in my mouth, or calling me at all hours of the day or night to ask something that just couldn't wait.

But in that tiny bathroom, with its low, jockey-size doors, I could finally escape.

Sitting there, I realized I'd spent years *adding*—piling on more responsibilities, more pressure, more expectations—without stopping to ask whether I *should*. I had the title, the "success," the income, and the respect of my clients and peers. All the things a business owner wants.

But I didn't have the one thing I desperately needed most: *freedom*.

MY "WHY" CHANGED

That moment marked the start of a shift. I knew I couldn't keep going the way I had been. I needed to redefine what success looked like for me and figure out how to make our business *work for me*, not the other way around. What I experienced that day wasn't about burnout—it was about the realization that success without intention isn't true success. The same traits that helped make our business successful—drive, resilience, and the ability to solve problems— were also trapping me.

In the early days of our practice, the way I got traction with clients was to be available to everybody, all the time. If you called me, I would pick up the phone no matter what time of the day or night it was.

I tolerated people texting me in the evening or calling me on my day off. I'm not proud to admit this, but the day after I gave birth to Emma, I was on the phone talking to a client about what they needed to do with their horse. (You know how it is with the second child, right?)

As one of my mentors once said, "You teach the behavior you tolerate!"

I taught my coworkers and clients that I was always available and that they needed me for everything. I said yes to every opportunity and every challenge.

I didn't think there was anything wrong with this at the time, though. I thought being available 24/7 was just part of being a successful business owner. You're busy. You're in demand. You do what it takes to make people happy and serve them well.

But somewhere along the way, it stopped feeling good. My priorities had shifted, but I'd been too busy to notice.

When I first started out, I was single. All I wanted was to be a great veterinarian. I wanted to own a business, make lots of money, and have all of the things I'd ever dreamed of.

Later, when I got married and started having kids, I also wanted to be a good spouse and parent. Like a lot of business owners who also happen to have responsibilities outside of work, I realized that I wanted more from life than just to be a great veterinarian.

My *why* had changed.

That happens to most of us because we almost never stop to reevaluate what really matters to us. It's a huge problem for business owners because we're so busy, we don't take time to pause and think about the deeper questions.

Why am I doing this? What do I want to get out of it? What kind of life do I want my business to support? And why do I want it?

Spoiler alert: If you don't figure it out, you might end up with a business you don't even like anymore.

For me, the wake-up call was realizing that my business wasn't working for me—in fact, the opposite was true. But once I got clear on what I wanted and *why*, I started looking at how my business could give me freedom and options, not just money.

> **ONCE YOU KNOW WHAT YOU WANT AND WHY YOU WANT IT, THE REST IS JUST LOGISTICS.**

FROM VET TO BUSINESS & EXIT STRATEGIST

I don't want to give the impression that just because I had a light bulb moment of clarity, things immediately turned around. Far from it. To run my business smarter instead of harder required learning—a lot of learning.

In fact, my transition from veterinarian to Business & Exit Strategist wasn't one of those cool and inspiring social media–worthy success stories. It was more like a shitshow involving a lot of mistakes, faceplants, and moments of sheer panic.

As my partners and I grew our practice, by necessity I became more involved in the business side of things. I realized I really enjoyed that part, but I also didn't have any formal business training. I was really good at being a veterinarian, but business? Was I really doing the right things?

After all, I'd become an entrepreneur by accident. So, I decided to do what I knew had worked for me in the past—get a degree. I took classes and got my MBA online while continuing to do everything else.

While I wouldn't recommend my approach to anyone, my studies did help me realize that our business needed to change if we wanted it to survive long term. There were external forces at play, such as regulatory changes and other economic factors, that we couldn't control but needed to anticipate.

We also had internal challenges, such as associates who weren't that interested in business ownership, that would affect how we could eventually exit the business.

Not to mention, our financials had been neglected, vendor pricing had not been renegotiated, and we'd never updated any of our operating agreements (even after the departure of some partners). The list went on and on.

In the short term, I knew I needed to find ways to stop being a bottleneck. In the long term, we needed a way to eventually transfer ownership if we wanted to get any real value from our sweat equity.

I focused on turning our business into the cash cow it could be—without needing me or my partner for its continued success. We needed systems and processes, more leadership depth, and a way to build value that didn't require us to be at the center of things.

Once we got our business working properly and I stopped micromanaging everything—more on that later—we were able to explore options for transitioning ownership.

We eventually merged our practice with a group of other practices, where I had the opportunity to help acquire more veterinary practices. As part of this process, I met with many owners who wanted to sell their businesses, and those conversations were eye-opening.

Most of the businesses I evaluated weren't sellable—not because they weren't profitable, but because they were completely dependent on the owner. They were lifestyle businesses, designed to fund their owners' day-to-day lives, but without any systems, leadership depth, or transferable value.

It broke my heart to explain to these owners that the business they had poured their blood, sweat, and tears into—their "baby"—was worth little more than the value of its assets minus its liabilities.

They had essentially built themselves a very well-paying job, one that no one else could take over because it was too reliant on them. I hated having those conversations, but it opened my eyes to how widespread the problem is.

> **STATISTICS SHOW THAT ONLY AROUND 20 PERCENT TO 30 PERCENT OF BUSINESSES THAT GO TO MARKET ARE SUCCESSFULLY SOLD.[1]**

As a result, I started asking myself: *How can I help other business owners avoid these mistakes? How do I show them how to build something that's fun to run now and easy to sell later?*

---

1 https://www.forbes.com/sites/forbesfinancecouncil/2023/08/24/business-exit-planning-watch-for-these-blind-spots/

Those same questions were on my mind as I wrote *The Business Owner's Freedom Flywheel.*

You may have picked up this book because you know your business isn't as fun to run as it could be, and you're dreading getting it ready to sell when the time comes.

Please know that not only have I been where you are, I can help you get to where you want to go.

But before we get into the details of the Freedom Flywheel, I want to take a few moments in Chapter One to share a critical message you need to hear as we begin this journey: You can do this!

1 YOU CAN DO THIS!

2 **F**IX THE FIRES

3 **R**EVERSE ENGINEER YOUR PLAN

4 **E**MBRACE METRICS THAT MATTER

5 **E**STABLISH OWNER INDEPENDENCE

6 **D**RIVE GROWTH AND SCALABILITY

7 **O**PTIMIZE PROFITABILITY

8 **M**ULTIPLY YOUR VALUE

You Can
Do This!

CHAPTER ONE

YOU CAN DO THIS!

If there's one thing I know about you, it's this: You didn't achieve this level of success by accident.

You've earned every inch of progress with grit, determination, and probably more coffee than you'd like to admit. Sure, there were wins, a few lessons disguised as challenges, and maybe even a leap of faith or two that made your stomach drop.

But here you are.

And no matter how many plates you've got spinning in the air right now, you've got this. You can absolutely create a business that works for you—without feeling like it's calling the shots.

As a business owner, you signed up for the excitement of running your own show. But you also have to admit that it's a lot, always being the person everyone comes to.

When you're that busy, it can be hard to picture what might be possible. But just for a few moments, take yourself out of the day-to-day world of your business and dream.

LET'S IMAGINE SOMETHING DIFFERENT

Imagine this: Your alarm goes off in the morning, and instead of hitting snooze three times, you're actually excited to get out of bed.

I know, wild concept, right? But stay with me. You don't feel like you're walking into yet another day of putting out fires. You're not already bracing yourself for the fifteenth email labeled "URGENT" before you've had your coffee.

Instead, you wake up energized—maybe even happy—because your business doesn't just function; it flows.

You've got a team that actually runs like the well-oiled machine you always dreamed of, which means you're no longer holding the operation together with duct tape and sheer willpower.

Customers? They're not just satisfied; they're thrilled, and their drama-free energy actually makes your day better.

And here's the kicker: Financially, you're killing it. Bills? Paid. Profits? Growing. Retirement? It's no longer a dream. You're living the life you've worked so hard for and planning for a future that excites you.

Oh, and let's add this little cherry on top: If someone knocked on your door and offered to buy your business tomorrow, you wouldn't be scrambling to pull it together. You'd be ready—calm, confident, and ready to say "yes" on *your* terms.

Sounds like a pipe dream? It's not. This dream is absolutely within reach. You're not here because your business is failing. You're here because you want it to be better.

And that's exactly what we're going to accomplish together.

But don't just take my word for it. Let me introduce you to a couple of business owners who had every appearance of success on the outside but were secretly stuck in the hamster wheel of busy. They made the leap from running on fumes to running their business with freedom and intention.

If they can do it, so can you.

THE ARCHITECT WHO WAS THE BOTTLENECK

One of my clients was an architect who seemed to have it all together—on the surface.

He loved his work, drove a nice car, and lived in a beautiful neighborhood. But behind the scenes, things were not as they seemed. He hadn't saved enough for his future, his business wasn't set up to be sellable, and—big surprise—everything had to go through him.

Every decision, every approval—he was the Grand Central Station of his own company. And yes, he knew he was the bottleneck, but he had no idea how to fix it.

His accounts receivable was a mess, and there wasn't a plan for what would happen when he was ready to step away.

We started by clarifying his long-term goals and mapping out a plan to increase the value of his business. Then came the hard part: delegation. Slowly but surely, he began handing off tasks, trusting his team, and building systems that didn't involve him being in the middle of everything.

The payoff? He finally took those RV trips he'd been dreaming about, started saving for his future, and even began exploring potential buyers for his business. For the first time, his business supported his life instead of running it.

THE CASH-PRINTING BUSINESS WITHOUT A PLAN

Then there were the partners in a wildly profitable business. On paper, everything looked amazing—they were practically printing money. But there was one big problem: They didn't have an exit strategy.

They realized that if they didn't figure it out, they might have to just shut things down one day and walk away from years of hard work (and cash flow).

We worked together to get their operations running like clockwork, documented the value of their business, and positioned it for a sale. The result? They didn't just save their business—they sold it for more than they ever expected to.

These clients weren't billionaires with unlimited resources. They were regular business owners who decided they were done with the chaos and ready for a change.

And guess what? If they could do it, so can you.

Before we get into the details of how you can make this happen in your own business, let's take a quick look at three important questions— Why me?, Why you?, and Why now?—and then we will explore what the Freedom Flywheel is all about.

WHY ME?

You might wonder why I'm even the right person to bring you this message. After all, I didn't get it all right the first time around. In fact, I made a lot of mistakes.

Those mistakes are precisely what make me uniquely qualified to write this book.

> **FOR YEARS, I WAS SO BUSY WORKING *IN* MY BUSINESS THAT I DIDN'T WORK *ON* IT. THE MONEY KEPT COMING IN, AND I THOUGHT THAT WAS ENOUGH.**

Then the market crash of 2008 hit, and I realized working harder wasn't going to solve the problem. I had to work smarter.

I also learned the hard way about the importance of planning for an exit. While we eventually sold to a larger aggregator, I know that if I'd started planning earlier, I could have secured better terms and more value.

My experiences as a business owner, buyer, seller, and strategist shaped the Freedom Flywheel framework you're about to learn.

WHY YOU?

This book is for business owners who want more—more profit, more freedom, and more time to focus on what really matters.

If you're someone who:

- takes action and responsibility for your success
- dreams bigger but wants strategic growth— not growth for growth's sake

- is willing to learn from mistakes and adapt to new strategies

- is overwhelmed by the day-to-day grind and wants less stress and more freedom, and

- wants to run a business, not let it run their life

… then you're in the right place!

Now, you might be thinking, *This sounds great for someone running a big, fancy business, but what about me?* I get it. Not everyone fits the same mold, and that's okay.

Whether you're the owner of a business knocking on the door of $5 million, you've consistently been hitting $10 million, or you're almost to $50 million, this book can help. And I just might be the person you've been looking for!

Here is just a sampling of what you'll learn in the pages ahead:

- How to take more time off without worrying your business will collapse the second you step away.

- How to reduce stress, free up time in your day-to-day, and actually grow—even if you already feel like you're running on fumes.

- Practical, doable ways to make your business more efficient, profitable, and less of a constant headache.

This isn't about adding more to your already full plate—it's about clearing some space so you can actually enjoy what you're building. Wherever you're starting from, this framework will help you to create a business that works for you, not the other way around.

WHY NOW?

Let me share a few simple business realities that make this book urgently needed.

The first reality, as I mentioned earlier, is you *will* exit your business someday. You may do it vertically or horizontally. But there is a 100 percent chance it will happen.

In fact, there are five common reasons people exit their business unexpectedly. We call them the "5 Ds":

- Death,

- Disability,

- Divorce (being forced to sell your business),

- Disagreement (partnership disagreements are very common), and

- Distress (due to market conditions, regulatory changes, or elements beyond your control).

If you don't have a plan, your business may not survive your departure, let alone have any value.

The second business reality is that many entrepreneurs believe they can't get away from their business for any length of time because they're afraid it will fall apart.

Without the right team and structure in place, the owner wears all the hats in the company. They often struggle to take time off, let alone take a real vacation. A study published in the *Harvard Business Review* showed that 96 percent of U.S. professionals say they need flexibility, but only 47 percent actually have it.[1]

Let's be honest. Even if you love your work, you need to have space for the other aspects of your life. You need better systems so you can breathe and enjoy the life you deserve.

And the third business reality is that just 30 percent of family businesses make it to the second generation, and the numbers decrease with each generation.[2] So if you're thinking of passing your business on to the next generation—perhaps a family member or a long-term employee—start planning now.

---

1 https://hbr.org/2018/06/96-of-u-s-professionals-say-they-need-flexibility-but-only-47-have-it

2 https://www.im-financial.com/blog/the-generational-decline-why-success-becomes-harder-with-each-generation-i

> **THE SOONER YOU START PLANNING,
> THE MORE OPTIONS YOU'LL HAVE—
> AND THE MORE LIKELY YOUR BUSINESS
> WILL GIVE YOU THE LIFE YOU WANT,
> BOTH *NOW* AND *LATER*.**

What can you do to avoid the pitfalls that trip up so many owners? I'm so glad you asked.

THE FREEDOM FLYWHEEL

The Freedom Flywheel is a simple, actionable framework designed to help you build a business that's fun to run now and easy to sell later.

The concept of a flywheel is powerful: It builds momentum over time, becomes self-sustaining, and keeps turning with less effort. In this same way, each of the seven elements of the Freedom Flywheel builds on the last, creating energy and progress.

Here is an overview, and I promise we'll dive deeply into each element in the chapters to come:

- *Fix the Fires:* Remove the obstacles slowing you down.

- *Reverse Engineer Your Plan:* Define your destination and work backward.

- *Embrace Metrics That Matter:* Focus on what truly drives success.

- *Establish Owner Independence:* Build systems and leadership so your business can run without you.

- *Drive Growth and Scalability:* Expand strategically for long-term impact.

- *Optimize Profitability:* Ensure every effort maximizes results.

- *Multiply Your Value:* Position your business as a scalable, sellable asset.

This isn't just theory—it's a methodology grounded in practical, tested strategies from someone who's been in the trenches. And it's not about someday off in the unforeseeable future. It's about building a business that works for you *now*.

In the next chapter, we'll tackle the fires stealing your time and energy. You'll learn how to create space to breathe, focus, and regain control, and best of all, you'll stop having to put out the same flames over and over again.

Let's get started. Your future, chaos-free business awaits!

Fix the
Fires

CHAPTER TWO

FIX THE FIRES

In your imagination, picture a boardroom full of a company's leaders. They're dissecting a spreadsheet projected onto the big-screen TV and debating projections like their lives depend on it. The tension is palpable.

Meanwhile, the office next to them is burning. Smoke is billowing out the door and seeping through the air vents. Huge orange flames are visibly licking at the glass doors of the boardroom.

The fire alarm has been going off for several minutes, but no one seems to notice, even though it's drowning out the person talking. A few people in the meeting start coughing due to the smoke.

Shockingly, they keep analyzing the numbers, oblivious to the fact that the building is about to go up in flames.

Sounds crazy, doesn't it? What company leaders—or what kind of people, for that matter—could possibly sit in a meeting with all that chaos and danger surrounding them? Yet, metaphorically, it happens every day in thousands of companies.

There are two different kinds of fires we're talking about. First, the everyday emergencies that crop up to steal your time—the day-to-day challenges you are unable to ignore.

Then there are the secondary fires: the things that, if left unattended, really could burn down your business. They are usually smoldering in the background and can ignite at any moment.

What you need are systems that allow you to focus on the real threats, instead of being in triage mode constantly.

That's why the first element in the Freedom Flywheel is "Fix the Fires." You can't build the business of your dreams based on chaos. Fires demand your attention, drain your energy, and keep you from focusing on the big picture.

> **IF YOU WANT FREEDOM AND CONTROL, YOU FIRST HAVE TO PUT OUT THE FIRES.**

Not every problem is a fire. Fires are the recurring, urgent issues, and sometimes embarrassing problems that refuse to die on their own. They tend to grow bigger and nastier the longer you ignore them. These fires don't just steal your time—they steal your momentum. And if you don't address them, they'll burn through your resources and your sanity.

Instead, you can free up time, energy, and bandwidth with some strategic fixes. It's not about perfection (for the perfectionists in the room)—it's about prioritizing what matters most and taking action.

Let's look at three ways to Fix the Fires: *practicing triage, paying to make the pain go away,* and *creating space for strategic thinking.*

PRACTICE TRIAGE

When I worked at the racetrack, chaos was my normal.

Here's a typical moment in my day. I'd have one horse who suddenly had a bellyache and was clearly uncomfortable. Another horse apparently had had a sore foot off and on over the past couple of days. And then there was always that one owner whose horse had been coughing occasionally for three weeks, but today was the day they finally decided it was a problem.

It was my job to assess the scene and answer these questions: Which issue is most urgent? Which one can wait? And which one might just be someone's overreaction?

Running a business is no different. Fires pop up everywhere. Your job is to figure out which deserve immediate action, and which can smolder a bit longer before they get doused.

Take a moment to ask yourself: What's stealing my time, energy, and focus? And more importantly, which of these things has the potential to do the most damage if left unattended?

Let's recap some of the usual suspects:

Risk: Unlike the obvious fires, unmanaged risk is like termites—you don't notice them eating away at the structure until the building begins to collapse. Mitigating risk isn't sexy, but addressing it is one of the cheapest and easiest ways to immediately increase the value and sustainability of your business.

Conduct a risk audit, including reviewing insurance policies and contracts, looking for compliance landmines, and creating contingency plans.

Cash Flow Crunches: Ever feel like your bills are due but your cash is playing a game of hide-and-seek? Maybe you've taken on a big client and had to front-load expenses—supplies, payroll, infrastructure—only to wait months before the money starts rolling in? Been there. It's not just frustrating; it's business threatening.

I learned this lesson the hard way:

> **PLANNING FOR CASH FLOW CRUNCHES DURING GROWTH SPURTS ISN'T JUST SMART—IT'S SURVIVAL.**

Bottlenecks: These traffic jams in your business processes leave clients waiting, blow past deadlines, and raise stress levels. Or employees are frustrated because they can't do their job well. We'll get more into this in Chapter Five.

Sometimes it's an issue outside your control, like a supply chain problem. But whether it's internal or external, bottlenecks need a solution—not an excuse.

People Problems: Toxic employees. Misaligned roles. Constant drama. It's exhausting at best, revenue draining at worst.

I recently worked with a client who had an employee who was less of a team player and more of a grenade with the pin pulled. He'd known for a while that this person had to go, but the thought of the confrontation (and paperwork) kept him stuck.

Problematic people drain your time, energy, and morale faster than you realize. Once my client finally took action, he couldn't believe the difference. The rest of the team stepped up, and the business began running more smoothly almost immediately.

You're not here to be a superhero. You can't fix every problem all at once. But you can focus on the fires that pose the greatest threat to your business's stability and momentum.

Key Takeaway: Don't try to fight every fire at once. Start with those that, if left burning, will cause the most damage. That's how you move from chaos to control—and from survival to strategy.

PAY TO MAKE THE PAIN GO AWAY

One of the hardest shifts we can make is moving from working *in* your business to working *on* it.

We all understand the concept—it's been around forever. But putting it into practice is a whole different thing than just knowing about it.

The basic concept is simple (yet oddly difficult): *You shouldn't be doing everything.* You need to identify the things only you can do, then delegate or outsource the rest to someone else.

I once had a client who would often work the phones at the front desk of her company. She didn't love doing it and wasn't even particularly good at it—it had simply become a habit. She could easily have had someone else doing it! She just never stopped to consider the alternatives.

We all fall into these ruts. We keep doing things out of habit or guilt, or even some weird sense of pride. Maybe we think it's easier and less time-consuming if we just do the thing ourselves.

I've been there. I remember being a new mom and working 24/7, doing "all the things." One of my business partners (a seasoned business veteran whose kids were grown) asked me, "Dawn, do you have a housekeeper? Who does your laundry?"

I blinked. "Um, me?"

"Why?" he said with a look on his face like I'd just confessed to a terrible sin. "Can't you afford to hire someone? That doesn't seem like a good use of your time."

I could definitely afford it, but it never occurred to me that I *should*. Let me tell you, the first time I walked into my freshly cleaned house to find order restored, the laundry done, and the bedsheets crisp and clean, it was life-changing!

That's just one small example. There are all sorts of "pains" you can pay someone to make go away.

Figure out what tasks you dread doing. Maybe it's accounting, marketing, or posting on social media. Maybe it's writing content. Maybe you need a social media assistant. Or like the former client I mentioned, maybe hire someone to answer the phones or do other administrative work. Perhaps it would be a huge relief to turn your financials and/or payroll over to a firm that specializes in it.

Think of it this way: Whatever you dislike doing (or is a waste of your precious time) is likely thrilling to someone else. Let them shine instead of making yourself do *everything*.

When you look at highly successful people, they are typically not doing things they find tedious or low-value. They have learned to outsource the pain points in their lives and businesses. They aren't successful because they work more hours than everyone else—their success is a result of them *spending their time where it counts.*

Sometimes business owners don't do this, though, because they're afraid of what others will think. I worked with a business owner who pushed back on this idea. She said, "I wouldn't want my employees to think that I feel those kinds of tasks are beneath me."

This is not about something being "beneath" you. It's about having the right mindset, knowing you only have so much time in your day. You need to use it on the most high-value tasks possible.

This isn't about ego, it's about math. If you can pay someone $20 an hour to handle tasks while you use that time to work on $200-an-hour problems, guess what? You just made $180 an hour. Where could you be making more money if your time was freed up from doing tasks you could easily delegate or outsource?

How to Track Your Time

Do you really know where your time is going? I recommend performing an activity audit.

> **EVERY DAY FOR TWO WEEKS, TRACK, IN THIRTY-MINUTE INCREMENTS, HOW YOU SPEND YOUR TIME.**

Write down what you're doing and for how long. The results will probably shock you.

Why? Because you'll likely find that you're spending vast amounts of time on things that you could easily—and cheaply—outsource to others.

We'll dive deeper into this process later in the book, but for now, let's keep it simple. Think of this as a quick start guide to reclaiming your brainpower:

Step 1: Identify one or two tasks to delegate immediately.

Maybe it's the bookkeeping that makes you want to cry, the endless social media posting, or the mountain of emails that never stop multiplying. Hand it off. Seriously, you have better things to do—like plotting world domination or binge-watching your favorite show guilt-free (depending on the day).

Step 2: Outsource or automate anything repetitive.

If you're still manually scheduling appointments and meetings, approving every little thing, or tracking receipts in a shoebox, it's time to find a better way. Technology and outsourcing can streamline these tasks and free up your time for more important priorities.

Step 3: Eliminate tasks that aren't serving you.

Some tasks don't need to be delegated or automated—they just need to disappear altogether. If you've been spending hours on things that don't actually move the needle or add value, it's time to let them go. Ask yourself: Does this task actually contribute to progress or profit (or is it legally required of my business)? If not, it's time to cross it off your list for good.

Key Takeaway: Some pains are worth paying to make go away because the return on investment (ROI) on your mental clarity is priceless.

CREATE SPACE FOR STRATEGIC THINKING

This is where the magic starts to happen. The whole goal of practicing triage and making the pain go away is to free you from low-value tasks so you have the time to think strategically.

Let me be blunt: You are never going to change anything if you're constantly stuck in the grind. You can't think creatively, dream big, or plot your next big move until you have the time and space to think.

One of the reasons good business coaching works so well is not because the coach has magic answers. It's because the process forces you to pause, asks the right questions, and gives you the space to consider them before answering them for yourself. Great coaches make sure you aren't just thinking about the tasks at hand. They're challenging you to look up and see the bigger picture.

> **IT'S IMPOSSIBLE TO THINK OUTSIDE THE BOX WHEN YOU'RE STUCK INSIDE THE CHAOS. THAT'S WHY CARVING OUT TIME AND SPACE FOR REFLECTION MATTERS.**

One of my mentors encouraged me to schedule thinking time every week. My response was, "Dude, I can't even get five minutes of peace without literally hiding out in the toilet."

He said, "You don't have time *not* to do this. Put it on your calendar."

I rolled my eyes. "I don't even use a calendar. I'm running around just putting out fires all the time."

He pushed back. "Okay. What time is it now? Four p.m. on Thursday. Every Thursday at four p.m., you're going to stop whatever you're doing. No exceptions. Put it aside so you can think. I don't want you solving problems. Instead, I want you to think about all the possibilities."

That conversation changed everything. What he was getting at was the importance of mindset. Scheduling dedicated strategic thinking time ultimately allowed me to make major moves like merging our business with other practices and eventually, launching my consulting business.

Until I made the space, I couldn't see the forest for the trees. But when I started to create space in my life for strategic thinking, everything started to change.

I used to think I was crushing it. I wasn't just a good doer—I was a *super doer*! If being busy was an Olympic sport, I'd have taken home gold, silver, and bronze. I worked hard, I worked fast, and I got a lot done.

But I wasn't actually getting anywhere. It was like running on a treadmill—lots of effort, zero forward momentum. It turns out that being busy doesn't guarantee progress, only exhaustion.

When I started creating space—giving myself one hour a week—to think strategically, everything shifted. I stopped just reacting to the day-to-day and started replacing chaos with clarity.

Key Takeaway: When you schedule strategic thinking time, you create a habit of looking at the view from thirty thousand feet and seeing all the possibilities. That's where real progress happens.

✿ ✿ ✿

Now that we've focused on fixing the fires in your business and you have some practical steps to move forward, let's turn our attention to something you can do when you free up time and energy for strategic thinking: reverse engineer your plan. Turn the page to find out how.

Reverse
Engineer
Your Plan

CHAPTER THREE

REVERSE ENGINEER YOUR PLAN

We kicked off the Freedom Flywheel with "Fix the Fires" for a reason. It's impossible to think about big-picture strategy when you're dodging metaphorical flames.

A crisis—whether it's financial, personnel-related, or operational—sucks up all the oxygen in the room. The goal of fixing those fires was to give you the space to step back and start seeing your business with clarity.

Now that you've got that space, it's time to start thinking about your overall vision.

This is the tricky part, though. The reason people struggle with vision is because it's hard to see past the reality of where you are right now.

That was always the challenge for me when I bought into my practice. It was a well-established business and they had been doing things the same way for a long time. It was hard to make meaningful changes because of the resistance I encountered.

I see this with business owners all the time. They'll say,

> **"YOU DON'T UNDERSTAND—YOU CAN'T DO THAT IN MY BUSINESS. IT JUST WON'T WORK."**

Translation: They're so used to the way things *are* that they can't imagine how they *could be*. All they can think about is how it's been done or how they're doing it now.

Most of the time, they're successful on some level. If it ain't broke, don't fix it, right? But remember, what got you *here* won't necessarily take you *there*.

That's why reverse engineering your plan is so critical. Lots of business owners are successful, but that doesn't necessarily mean it happened on purpose.

You don't want to leave *your* success to chance, so you've got to start with the end in mind, as Stephen Covey so brilliantly wrote about in *The 7 Habits of Highly Successful People*.

In this chapter we'll look at three keys to accomplishing that: *clarifying your vision and purpose, doing a brutal facts analysis,* and *mapping the journey.*

CLARIFY YOUR VISION AND PURPOSE

Terms like "vision" and "purpose" can feel vague. They sound like something you'd hear at a TED Talk right before the speaker launches into an inspiring story about climbing Mount Everest barefoot.

In theory at least, vision and purpose are the big ideas that guide our lives. However, most of us don't spend much time deliberately thinking about them.

We power through from year to year, decade to decade, wondering why we don't feel more successful or fulfilled.

But once we get clear on them, vision and purpose are like a GPS for our life and business.

What's Your Vision?

Think of vision as, well, an actual vision—something you see unfold like a movie on a giant screen. Imagine watching a preview of your future life where everything turns out just like you want it. You're the producer, director, and star of this film (and probably the lighting crew since entrepreneurs do it all), so dream big.

Most business owners hold back when it comes to vision. They'll say something vague like, "I want my company to grow." That's nice, but it's not a vision, it's a vague hope. Instead, paint a clear, vivid picture. "I want my company to double in revenue and to have locations in three countries over the next three years."

> **THE SPECIFICS MATTER.**
> **DON'T PLAY SMALL; CREATE A VISION**
> **BIG ENOUGH THAT IT FEELS**
> **A LITTLE UNCOMFORTABLE.**

Your vision is *yours*. Mentors, coaches, and authors (like me!) can help you brainstorm the possibilities, but no one can define your vision for you.

You have to *own* it.

What About Purpose?

Purpose is tied to your vision but it's not the same thing. If vision is about where you want to go, purpose is about why you're going there. It's what makes all the hard work, late nights, and tough decisions worth it.

Your purpose may be tied directly to your business. Maybe you want to provide jobs for your community, solve a problem no one else is addressing, or leave a legacy.

Or, your purpose might lie outside of your business. Maybe you want to spend more time volunteering, you dream of taking your grandkids on epic vacations (and actually having the energy to keep up with them), or you want to donate a big, show-stopping check to your favorite charity.

Whatever it is, that's your purpose.

And if your business isn't your life's passion, that's okay too. Plenty of people find themselves running businesses they didn't exactly choose. Maybe you inherited the role, fell into it by circumstance, or it just seemed like a good idea at the time.

Sometimes the purpose of your business is simply to provide the financial resources and freedom to allow you to pursue your passions. You don't have to intend to be the biggest or the best. Your purpose can be tailored so that it perfectly fits *you*.

Know Your Values

It's always best to make sure you know what your values are because they're the foundation for everything else.

When you think about what is most important to you in life right now, can you narrow it down to the top three things? When you go through this exercise, you may be surprised at how hard it is to get clarity on your values. I usually suggest you start by going through your values on a personal level.

Then ask yourself what you believe the core values of your business are. Are your personal core values in alignment with the core values of your business? They don't have to be the same, but they need to be able to coexist in harmony, or it won't feel good to you.

It's also important to remember to review your values periodically throughout your life, especially when you experience major changes. You may recall my story about how my priorities and what I valued changed after I became a parent, but I didn't pay attention and it got uncomfortable after a while.

If your business doesn't allow you to live in alignment with your personal values, you will always feel a disconnect.

GET MY "VET YOUR VISION" EXERCISE INCLUDED IN THIS BOOK'S BONUSES AT: PRODUCTIVEPRESSURE.COM/FLYWHEEL

The bottom line is that if you start thinking about your vision, and how everything ties into that, the path forward becomes much clearer.

Key Takeaway: Without a clear vision, you're just spinning your wheels. Without a purpose, you won't have the motivation to keep pushing when things get hard. And they will get hard!

DO A BRUTAL FACTS ANALYSIS

Once you have an idea of *what* you want and *why* you want it, you have to get super clear on where you are right now.

It might be painful. That's why I use the word "brutal." You're going to delve into not just your business finances—you're pulling back the curtain on everything. That includes your personal life and financial situation, even the parts you've been avoiding.

This is hard, especially as business owners, because we tend to wrap our identities up in what we do. If our business is doing well, we're a success. If it's struggling, we feel like we're failing.

This process is going to push some of those buttons. If you do this right, it may hurt, but it's going to be worth it.

You'll want to include all of your professional advisors—your accountant, financial planner, estate attorney—in this process. You'll need their help to gather all of the information you need for your brutal facts analysis. You're shooting for a completely transparent, no BS assessment of where you and your business stand at this moment in time.

You should include a business valuation, a review of your personal finances and your financial plan, consider your estate plan and associated tax strategies, as well as a review of any existing contracts and agreements.

This can be a little overwhelming, which is why I recommend professional help.

As a Business & Exit Strategist, I work with my clients' other trusted advisors to integrate all of that information into a cohesive plan. This is my superpower—I'm like a quarterback for the team. I don't block or tackle, I just support everyone else in their role, make sure the game plan is clear, and that we're all aiming for the same goal line.

Without that level of coordination, it can be difficult to see the full picture. Once you have this, it will be easier for you to understand what you need to accomplish to reach your goals.

If you don't have this information, you really don't know where you're starting from, so it's hard to plan the course for where you want to go. You need to know the gap between your vision and your current reality.

I worked with a business owner once who was convinced he needed $6 million to retire comfortably. He was grinding himself into the ground chasing this number, sacrificing time with his family and his health.

When we finally sat down with his financial planner for the brutal facts analysis, it turned out he needed only $5 million to live the life he wanted. That one-million-dollar difference changed everything. Knowing the real target allowed us to create a solid plan to get him there. Suddenly, his goals felt achievable. He could see the finish line.

The lesson? When you get clear on the gap—whether it's a wealth gap, a value gap, or just the gap between your expectations and reality—everything else becomes logistics. You can stop guessing and start planning.

Here's what I recommend you do next:

1. ***Gather Your Team:*** You're going to need your accountant, financial planner, and lawyer. If you don't have these people, get them. You wouldn't try to rebuild an engine without a mechanic, and you shouldn't try to untangle your financial situation without experts.

2. ***Get Your Business Valuation:*** This is where you find out what your business is *actually* worth—not what you think it's worth after scrolling through social media and seeing someone claim they sold a company for 10x revenue. This can be sobering, but it's a critical step.

3. ***Do a Gap Analysis:*** This includes the following:

   - *Wealth Gap:* What do you have now, and what do you need to live the life you want?

   - *Value Gap:* How much is your business worth today, and how much does it need to be worth to meet your financial goals and close your wealth gap?

   - *Purpose Gap:* Is your business aligned with your personal values and purpose, or is it just a means to an end? Having clarity on this may determine what you want your role in the business to be going forward—if you even want to continue to work *in* the business.

Key Takeaway: Understanding where you are today is the foundation for getting where you want to go.

MAP THE JOURNEY

Once you've clarified your vision and purpose (where you're going and why) and have done a brutal facts analysis (where you are), the next logical step is *how* to get from here to there. It's time to map the journey.

This is where you come up with a concrete plan to get the freedom and financial security you want, both now and later.

As a business owner, it's easy to fall into the "someday" trap—feeling like you have to grind away for years or decades, toughing it out and sucking it up until you can *finally* retire and enjoy your life at some undetermined point in the future.

But what if you could enjoy life both in the future *and* right now? What if you could have freedom *now* instead of deferring it for thirty years?

We'll get into the specifics of how to do this in later chapters. But for now, let's work on reverse engineering your plan from there to here.

Assuming you didn't make any adjustments to your vision or purpose after completing your brutal facts analysis, the next step is just about connecting the dots.

Here's where the reverse engineering comes in. You need to start with where you want to end up and plot the journey back to where you are today.

For example, five years from now the owner of a $4 million business wants to sell it for $6 million. Cool. So, what does it need to be worth three years from now? One year from now? What needs to happen in each of those times frames to support that growth?

Once you know what needs to happen in the next year, break it down further into ninety-day (quarterly) sprints. During each sprint, you'll focus on certain goals that will drive the results you want and need. From there you'll create action plans and assign ownership and accountability to team members.

The more granular you get, the more likely you are to be successful. At the end of the day, most strategic plans fail because while they might look cool, they lack implementation and a rhythm for consistent accountability.

I never said this way easy! It's anything but. However, just like you've probably noticed, the things in life—and business—that are worth the most, are often the hardest. And they're absolutely worth it.

Key Takeaway: Once you're clear on your vision and why, the rest is just logistics. Your plan for the journey will guide every decision and action.

✿ ✿ ✿

In the next chapter, we'll dive into one of my favorite keys of the Freedom Flywheel—embracing metrics that matter.

It's easy to get distracted by all the data and numbers available to us in our business. But now that you're armed with a way to fix the fires and reverse engineer your plan, it's time to get a bit more granular and take a look at your most important metrics. That's the topic of Chapter Four.

Embrace
Metrics
That Matter

CHAPTER FOUR

EMBRACE METRICS THAT MATTER

Welcome to the third element of the Freedom Flywheel: metrics. Wait, don't roll your eyes just yet.

I know metrics don't sound exciting. If this were a movie, it would be the part where someone pulls out a spreadsheet and half the audience walks out.

Stick with me, though. This is one of the most important chapters in this entire book. Why? In order to successfully follow your reverse engineered plan, you need to measure your progress regularly along the way. And without mastering this, you won't reach your goals—and you wouldn't even know if you did!

This doesn't mean just tracking your numbers, it means identifying and monitoring the *right* metrics for your business.

When you focus on the *right* numbers instead of getting distracted by the *wrong* numbers, they can tell you the real story of your business. They can show you where to focus your energy so you can have more freedom, more profitability … and, most importantly, more *fun*!

So, let's dive into three key concepts that will make this both actionable and (dare I say it again) fun: *ignoring vanity metrics, focusing on the right metrics*, and *then taking appropriate action*.

IGNORE VANITY METRICS

Let's start with a confession: I've fallen for vanity metrics before. Who hasn't at some point?

These are metrics designed to make you look and feel good, rather than actually being helpful or relevant. Think of vanity metrics like the social media highlights reel of your business: They look impressive at first glance, but they don't tell the whole story.

A lot of people love to focus on revenue—specifically, top-line revenue. That money your business is bringing in every month, every quarter, every year, whatever.

People love bragging about revenue. "We're an eight-figure business!" But revenue is just the money coming in; it doesn't necessarily mean you're keeping any of it. Even if your business is pulling in $10 million, if your expenses are $9,500,000 that's not a great ROI.

If you have a highly efficient business that's lean but you're only making high six figures, your business might actually be worth more than a seven-figure business that's burning through cash and has crazy high expenses.

Another vanity metric can be profit. Now, of course, profit matters—it's a key indicator of success. But it doesn't necessarily mean that your business is *valuable*. And it definitely doesn't guarantee your cash flow is good.

On paper, your profit might look solid—your income is greater than your expenses. But there are all sorts of dynamics that can make things tricky.

For example, if your business relies heavily on accounts receivable, it might look like you have "earned" a lot of money. But if people haven't paid you, that cash isn't in your pocket.

You'll be paying taxes on that money, even if you haven't actually received it—and that's the kind of cash flow crunch that can sink a business. Even one that looks profitable on paper. This is why it's important to look at metrics that actually matter to you and your business.

It's easy to get too focused on the wrong financial metrics, but it's also easy to focus on other metrics that don't necessarily correlate with the value of your business.

Another metric a lot of business owners want to show off is their "team." Some owners love the appearance of success and the sense of energy and confidence that comes from hiring people.

However, the number of people on your payroll has no direct connection to the value of your business. In fact, it often means more expenses and more headaches, and usually there is a gap between bringing them on board and the income that will (hopefully and eventually) result from their contributions.

Vanity metrics aren't just harmless distractions. They can actively lead you astray. Focusing on the wrong numbers can lead to wasting time, energy, and resources on things that don't matter. They can also give you a false sense of security by making you feel like all is well … when it's not.

Sounds pretty simple, right? But you'd be surprised how many owners fall into this trap.

Key Takeaway: The wrong metrics waste your time and energy. Focus on the numbers that drive value, not just revenue and profits.

FOCUS ON THE RIGHT METRICS

Not all metrics are created equal. Some are necessary for making smart decisions, while others just clutter your dashboard (more on that below). The key is to focus on the right numbers.

If vanity metrics aren't the answer, what should you be focusing on? The metrics that truly matter depend on your specific business, but there are a few things to consider:

Leading vs. Trailing Metrics: Trailing metrics, like revenue and profit, tell you what's already happened. Leading metrics such as customer inquiries, website traffic, or sales pipeline activity give you insight into what's coming next. A balanced focus on both leading and trailing metrics ensures you're proactive rather than reactive.

OKRs and KPIs: Objectives and Key Results (OKRs) and Key Performance Indicators (KPIs) are essential tools for aligning your team around measurable goals. While KPIs track *ongoing performance* in specific areas, OKRs help you set ambitious, *time-bound objectives*. For example, a KPI might track monthly sales growth, while an OKR might set a goal to increase sales by 25 percent in the next quarter.

Some universal metrics to consider tracking:

Revenue Growth Rate: Is your business growing or dying? We're going to talk more about growth in Chapter Six, but monitoring this can help you assess the impact of your sales strategies, customer demand, and market conditions. Sustainable growth is also a key factor in maximizing value.

EBITDA (Earnings Before Interest, Taxes, Depreciation, and Amortization): It's the go-to profitability metric for buyers because it focuses only on what the business actually earns from operations. It's a great snapshot of whether your business is profitable, scalable, and valuable.

Operating Cash Flow: If revenue is the heart of your business, cash flow is the blood. It's what keeps the lights on and the doors open. Are you collecting payments on time? Are you holding too much inventory? Cash flow metrics tell you how well your business is running day-to-day.

Customer Lifetime Value (LTV): How much revenue does the average customer bring in over the course of their relationship with you? This number helps you understand the long-term value of your customer base and informs decisions about marketing and retention.

Customer Acquisition Cost (CAC): How much are you spending to acquire a new customer? Compare this with your LTV to ensure you're not spending more to acquire customers than they're worth.

Profit Margins: Your profit margin tells you how efficiently your business turns revenue into profit. High revenue with low margins is a warning sign.

Employee Efficiency: Revenue or profit per employee can be a great way to measure whether your team is operating effectively. Are you getting the most out of your payroll investment?

How can you tell if your numbers are "good?" Start by taking a look at the benchmarks in your industry. Use sources like trade associations, financial and market research platforms, benchmarking tools and software, or an industry-savvy CPA. While they may not be exactly comparable to your business, they can usually give you a good indication of where you're doing well and where there's room for improvement.

Key Takeaway: Metrics should guide decisions, not overwhelm you. Track a few key numbers that align with your goals.

USE METRICS TO DRIVE ACTION

Now that you've determined the metrics you want to track and you have benchmarks to guide your analysis, it's time to break down your long-term goals into short-term actions. If your goal is to increase profit margins by 5 percent this year, what needs to happen this quarter? This month? This week? Next, add your targets to your reverse engineered plan from Chapter Three.

Then you'll want to create a dashboard (this could be as simple as a whiteboard or spreadsheet, or as sophisticated as a custom software application, depending on your needs). The dashboard allows you to have a current and clear view of the numbers that matter to you and your team.

Here's where the magic happens (or doesn't!).

> **METRICS ARE ONLY VALUABLE IF YOU USE THEM TO MAKE DECISIONS AND TAKE ACTION. WITHOUT ACTION, METRICS ARE JUST NUMBERS ON A PAGE.**

I once worked with a client who was obsessed with tracking their marketing metrics. They had spreadsheets full of data on click-through rates, social media engagement, and website traffic.

But when I asked how they were using that data, they admitted they weren't doing much with it. They were so busy analyzing that they hadn't made any changes to improve their marketing strategy.

This is what's known as analysis paralysis. It's easy to get so caught up in the data that you forget to use it to drive action.

Start by asking yourself questions like:

Where are the biggest leaks in my business? Metrics like cash flow and profit margins can help you identify inefficiencies or unnecessary expenses.

What's driving growth? Look at your most profitable products, services, or customer segments and focus your energy there.

What's holding me back? Metrics can highlight bottlenecks, whether it's a slow production process, low employee productivity, or high customer churn.

It's not just about you as the business owner understanding the metrics either—it's about getting that information out to your team. They need to be able to connect the vision with how they spend their time each day.

Delegate responsibility to your team for tracking and improving key metrics. Empower them to take ownership and be part of the solution. When everyone understands how their role impacts the bigger picture, it creates alignment and momentum. And it's your job as the leader to make that clear connection.

Key Takeaway: Metrics are only useful if they lead to action. Don't just track them—use them to transform.

✿ ✿ ✿

Remember, metrics are like the GPS of your business. They keep you on track and show you what steps to take next.

But it's essential to track *what matters*.

Don't get caught up in vanity metrics. Focus on the right numbers, take action on what they're communicating to you, and you'll be set up to become more independent from your business. That's the topic of Chapter Five.

Establish
Owner
Independence

CHAPTER FIVE

ESTABLISH OWNER INDEPENDENCE

Here is one of the great ironies of entrepreneurship: Many people decide to step away from a regular job in order to have the "freedom" of being a business owner. But in the end, they find that they're working much longer hours with more responsibility, more stress, and more risk.

You're supposed to be the one who's an owner, right? But many people who become entrepreneurs discover that the business owns *them*.

I want to help you establish independence from your business. If your business revolves around you, it's not scalable, sustainable, or ultimately as valuable as it could be.

It's a hard pill to swallow, I know. You've poured your blood, sweat, and tears into it. It's part of you. Many owners think of their business as their "baby."

> BUT YOUR BUSINESS IS NOT YOUR BABY. AND IF YOUR BUSINESS CAN'T RUN WITHOUT YOU, THEN IT'S NOT A BUSINESS, IT'S JUST A JOB—
> THE KIND OF JOB WHERE YOU'RE THE FIRST ONE IN, THE LAST ONE TO LEAVE, AND THE ONE WHO GETS THE CALL WHEN ANYTHING GOES WRONG.

While you may have lots of emotions and feelings tied to it, but I want to remind you that you are reading this book because you believe your business should be a financial asset that can be sold. Which also means it can increase in value and give you an impactful return.

In this chapter, we'll take a look at three interrelated issues to help you create a self-managing business: *dealing with the hard truth that you might be the bottleneck, understanding the roles of delegation, automation, and systems,* and *creating more leadership depth.*

ARE YOU THE BOTTLENECK?

"Bottleneck owners" believe they have to be the person making all the decisions and have their finger on the pulse of every part of their business.

If you're the bottleneck in your business, it doesn't mean you're a bad person or necessarily a bad leader. You're probably incredibly hard-working, dedicated, and passionate about your business. You've probably built it from the ground up and feel incredibly connected to every part of it. You care about it more than anyone else. And you may be stuck in the belief that if you don't do it yourself, it won't get done right.

Two types of owners fall into this category. One type is the bottleneck who hasn't realized it … yet. The second type knows they're the bottleneck, but they can't see any other way of doing things.

If neither of these describe you, congrats! You've done a great job pulling out of tasks that would eat up your time and energy—tasks that you've handed off to others so you can focus on more important things.

But maybe, like many people I work with, you feel you're somewhere in the middle. You don't think of yourself as a micromanager, but you know there are definitely some things you could delegate to others.

I know it's hard when you're caught up in the day-to-day rush of running your business. It's a challenge to find time to think about what you should get off your plate, and then execute a plan to make it happen.

Maybe you don't have the right people in the right roles, you don't know who to choose, or you don't think you can afford it. Maybe you've never learned how to delegate effectively.

For now, the most important thing is realizing that you need to give more thought to sharing the load so your business can start running without you. As they say, the first step to overcoming a problem is admitting you have one.

Key Takeaway: Admitting you're the center of everything is hard, but it's the first step toward creating freedom—for you and your business.

ELIMINATE, DELEGATE, AUTOMATE

Let me share a simple, game-changing framework for business owner independence: Eliminate, Delegate, Automate. These three practices form a cycle of productivity and freedom.

Once you put them into motion, they'll help you reclaim your time, refocus your energy, and run your business instead of letting it run you.

Step 1: Eliminate

Let's start with the easiest question: What doesn't need to exist in your workday at all?

This is where the activity audit is really important. If you already did it in Chapter Two, great! If not, here's a quick recap: Track everything you do for a week in thirty-minute increments.

No judgment, no editing—just log it all. Whether you're scrolling through your inbox, negotiating with vendors, or googling how to reset the Wi-Fi router for the third time this week, write it down.

Then take a hard look at the list and ask yourself: What's a total waste of time? What's not moving the needle in my business?

If you're being honest, you'll probably have to admit that there's some fluff on that list. Meetings that could've been emails. Tasks you're doing out of habit. Things you keep doing simply because you haven't really thought about why you need to be doing them at all.

The quickest win here is to eliminate the activities that aren't adding value. If you want to take it a step further, you can create a "not-to-do" list to remind you of the things you're committed to *not* doing anymore!

Step 2: Delegate

We talked about this in Chapter Two: Fix the Fires. After you've eliminated the fluff, identify what's left that does need to get done—but doesn't need to be done by you.

Let's face it: As business owners, we're pros at holding on to things we shouldn't. We say things like:

- "It's faster if I just do it myself."

- "No one else can do it as well as I can."
- "But what if they screw it up?"

Maybe we calculate how much time it will take us to train someone in the task and don't recognize those extra minutes will save hours in the months that follow. Someone else can do it, and the world won't end if they do it a little differently than you would. Delegation isn't about giving up control—it's about focusing on the work only you can do and letting your team (or external resources) handle the rest.

Not only will you free up time for yourself to work on higher-value projects, but you'll also allow others to learn new skills and take on more responsibility.

You can begin training your delegation muscles by starting with low-risk tasks. Try handing off repetitive admin work to an assistant, having someone else manage your email or customer inquiries, or delegating social media scheduling to a team member. Eventually, you will work up to outsourcing bigger projects that your team can't handle.

The goal isn't to offload your entire workload overnight—it's to chip away at the unnecessary and reclaim your bandwidth bit by bit.

> DELEGATION DONE WELL
> IS A GIFT TO BOTH YOU AND
> THE PERSON YOU SHARE THE
> RESPONSIBILITY WITH.

Step 3: Automate

Finally, automation. If a task can't be eliminated or delegated, ask yourself: Can it be automated?

Automation is your secret weapon for streamlining the repetitive tasks that eat away at your time. For example:

- **Micromanaging inventory and supply chain issues:** Use AI-driven systems to forecast demand and plan inventory levels. Automate vendor communication with software systems and let your well-trained staff resolve any problems.

- **Following up on sales leads:** Use your customer relationship management (CRM) system to automate lead nurturing and let your sales team focus on closing. That way *you* can focus on scaling!

- **Approving every IT purchase:** Use a procurement tool to set preapproved vendor lists and budget caps. Your time is better spent leveraging the tech ... to automate more tasks.

Start small. You don't need to go full tech-wizard with advanced software right away. Even basic automation—like automated scheduling or email automations—can save you hours every month. The key is to focus on automating tasks that drain your time or energy unnecessarily.

When you combine elimination, delegation, and automation, you create a system that frees you to focus on what truly matters—whether that's strategic planning, growing your business, or finally enjoying a guilt-free weekend.

This isn't just theory. I've seen it work for countless business owners. A couple of quick examples:

A client of mine was spending twelve hours a week manually invoicing clients. After delegating part of it to an assistant and automating the rest, they reclaimed that time to focus on building relationships with key clients and following up on new leads.

Within a few months, they saw a noticeable improvement in client retention and a steady increase in sales—proof that freeing up your time can drive meaningful growth where it matters most.

Another client was bogged down handling their own customer onboarding. By creating a streamlined process, delegating support to their team, and automating reminders, they cut onboarding time in half and improved customer satisfaction.

Every hour you free up is an hour you can reinvest in high-value work—or you can use it to just breathe a little easier.

Key Takeaway: Freedom doesn't come from doing everything—it comes from empowering others and creating systems that run themselves.

LEADERSHIP DEPTH

Understanding that you may be a bottleneck, then taking actions like eliminating, delegating, or automating tasks you shouldn't be doing are important steps toward going deeper as a leader.

But having a sustainable business requires more than just a great leader. It requires a culture of leadership throughout the organization. Take it from a recovering superhero—if you are the most important person in your business, not only is it not sustainable, but you also might be doing it wrong!

In an earlier chapter, I mentioned that I did a great job of whipping our business into shape. It was a lean, mean, well-oiled machine, with one exception. We had no leadership depth.

My partner and I were the rainmakers in our business, and proud of it! I was so integral to the day-to-day success of our business that I worked six to seven days a week. I was on call 24/7 until the day I gave birth to my first child.

Believe it or not, I went to work in labor because there was no one to cover for me that day. And when I came back three weeks later with a newborn and nanny in tow, I was a legend! And then I did it again with my second kid. (Of course, it was less impressive the second time around because I'd already shown it could be done.)

My "heroic" behavior meant that no matter how well the business ran when I was there, it fell apart when I wasn't. We had designed it that way. Looking back, I understand that it was a critical mistake.

As a business leader and owner, the goal is to be working *on* your business, doing high-level strategic thinking, more than working *in* your business.

When you're starting out, it's unavoidable to be doing all the things, but it's important *not* to get stuck in that role! Otherwise, you've bought yourself a job, not a business. That's exactly what I had done.

Have you ever been afraid to go on vacation because you were worried things might fall apart in your absence? Maybe you thought, *What if the team makes the wrong decisions? What if customers leave? What if there's some other crisis I haven't anticipated?*

Or maybe you've experienced this: Every time you do go on vacation you're exhausted by the preparation to leave. Then you try to spend a few days winding down while constantly checking your phone for messages and emails. Before your vacation is over, you're already dreading what will be waiting for you when you get back.

> **LEADERSHIP DEPTH IS ALL ABOUT BUILDING A SELF-MANAGING BUSINESS. ONE THAT DOESN'T NEED YOU TO FUNCTION.**

This means your team can make decisions, solve problems, and keep things running—even when you're not around.

It's about creating an environment where your people have autonomy over their roles, continuously improve their skills, and understand their purpose within the larger company vision.

Ultimately, your goal is to build a team that can operate and thrive without you. Because if your business grinds to a halt the moment you step away (or you're afraid it will), you don't have freedom.

You want to be replaceable.

> **THE MORE REPLACEABLE YOU ARE, THE STRONGER YOUR BUSINESS BECOMES.**

Here are some ways to create leadership depth:

Delegate Authority, Not Just Tasks: Don't keep all the decision-making power for yourself. Give your team the authority to make meaningful decisions and trust them to handle it.

Develop Future Leaders: Create a leadership succession plan. Invest in training, mentorship, and growth opportunities for your team. The more skilled and confident they are, the more they'll step up.

Document Processes: Create systems and standard operating procedures (SOPs) so that anyone can step into a role and know what to do. Think of it as "business insurance."

Test Your Team's Independence: Step away for a week. Then two. See how the business performs without you. Identify gaps and adjust. The goal is to make your absence a nonevent.

When you build leadership depth, a few amazing things happen:

First, your operations improve because everything doesn't depend on you.

Second, your risk decreases, which boosts the value of your business.

And third, you get to experience actual freedom—the kind where you can take a vacation without checking your email every hour.

An added bonus to all of this is as your team takes more ownership of your business, morale improves and profits grow.

Becoming more independent from your business gives you the ability to focus on what really matters—whether that's scaling to new heights or enjoying life outside of work.

And here's the reality check: 80 percent of businesses available for sale fail to sell. Buyers don't want to buy your job—they want to invest in a *self-sustaining*, scalable company that runs independently.

Key Takeaway: Building leadership depth is about more than just protecting your business— it's about creating a *self-managing business* that gives you freedom now and more value when you're ready to sell.

✿ ✿ ✿

This chapter might be the hardest one in the book to implement. Why? Because looking at your leadership requires a huge amount of honesty and self-reflection.

It's hard to admit that we might be holding our business back even though we want the best for it. Just like a parent who is facing an empty nest when their kids go off to college, every business owner has to realize that their "baby" needs to be separated from them at some point. It's a natural part of growth.

And the best part? When you intentionally become more independent from your business, not only can the business grow—you'll grow, too. It's an essential part of building more freedom into your life.

That independence also gives you the time, space, and energy to focus on driving greater growth for your business and yourself. We'll look at that next, in Chapter Six.

Drive Growth and Scalability

CHAPTER SIX

DRIVE GROWTH AND SCALABILITY

There's a saying in business that if you're not growing, you're dying. If you aren't focused on growth, then most likely you're going to shrink. It's almost impossible to maintain the status quo. It's like trying to balance on a bicycle without pedaling—eventually, you're going to tip over.

Why? Because things change. It becomes more expensive to deliver your product or your service. You lose clients. Your industry evolves. You go through a personal crisis of some kind.

That said, you don't just want to grow for the sake of getting bigger. Growth is accompanied by cost and risk, depending on how you're trying to grow.

> **THAT'S WHY GROWTH SHOULD BE STRATEGIC, SUSTAINABLE, AND ALIGNED WITH YOUR VISION.**

There are different types of growth. You can grow internally by taking on more customers, adding products or services to your core offerings, or exploring new verticals. External growth can come from acquiring other businesses like yours (potentially offering economies of scale) or those that give you a strategic advantage.

The possibilities are endless. But the bottom line is that sustainable growth is about doing the right things—not just doing more things. Growth should amplify your success, not your stress.

This chapter explores how to *build for scalability, prioritize what matters most,* and *use productive pressure to grow or scale without breaking.*

BUILD FOR SCALABILITY

One of the keys to scalability is having systems and processes in place. Once you have those, as well as clearly documented SOPs, you can easily add more to the system without needing a lot more people or financial input. It's much more efficient.

Scaling is different from growth. Growth is increasing output by adding resources proportionately. But with scaling, you're aiming for significantly increased output with your existing resources (or minimal additional resources).

Systems and processes are what allow you to create scale.

Spending time creating strong and efficient systems and processes makes your company more efficient, more sustainable, and more valuable. You should have systems and processes in place across all departments in your company.

Your systems, processes, and automations should all be thoroughly documented, usually through detailed written instructions and videos. They should be "live," readily accessible, and updated regularly by whoever uses them.

This is not just because it's more convenient for the people in the role now—SOPs are also incredibly valuable when it comes time to sell your company.

Write the SOPs in such a way that someone with very little training could perform the process or understand the system.

SOPs make it much easier to "plug and play" new employees into an existing system. This decreases training and onboarding costs and makes the business more sustainable.

If you don't leverage well-documented systems and processes in your business, not only is it difficult to grow, you'll end up with unnecessary bottlenecks.

I once had a client who kept pushing back against automating some of the bookkeeping practices in her business. She felt that if she wasn't writing the checks and delivering the receipts to the bookkeeper, she wouldn't be able to stay on top of the finances.

It was taking a lot of the owner's time and becoming a major drain on the business, which had grown to the point where it was impacting its ability to grow.

The owner's mindset was that the accountant wasn't able to do their job well, let alone do good tax accounting. The accountant didn't have timely financials since the owner would take all the receipts at the end of the month, write all her paper checks, and then report them when she received the bank statements.

As a result, they were always a couple of months behind in their bookkeeping. Not only was the owner spending too much time in this area, there was also a huge opportunity cost because of the constant bookkeeping delay. They couldn't make informed strategic decisions because their information was always a couple of months old.

All this requires a big mindset shift. You may have done things the same way for a long time. But spending a little time creating better systems and improving your mindset pays huge dividends later on. These are two areas I spend a lot of time on with my clients because they have an impact on every phase of the flywheel.

Key Takeaway: Scalability is about creating systems and capacity that can amplify your output without significantly increasing your costs or straining your resources.

FOCUS ON WHAT MATTERS MOST

The secret to *growing* the right way isn't about doing more—it's about doing the right things, at the right time, in the right ways.

Growth is not a badge of honor if it leaves you exhausted, overextended, and watching your business teeter on the edge of chaos. That's why the 80/20 Rule is your best friend. It says that 80 percent of your results come from 20 percent of your efforts, so your job is to identify which 20 percent is moving the needle and then laser-focus on it. This isn't about working harder—it's about working smarter.

Let's take a quick look at a few of the high-impact areas where growth can happen when you focus on what truly matters:

High-Value Customers: Think about your best customers—those who are profitable, easy to work with, and aligned with your business values.

They're probably the 20 percent that drives 80 percent of your revenue. What makes them such a great fit? How can you attract more clients like them?

Stop spreading your marketing efforts thin. Double down on finding and serving more of those customers. Build loyalty programs, ask for referrals, and create specialized offerings that cater to their specific needs.

Retention Over Acquisition: Customer acquisition is exciting, but let's face it—it's also expensive. Studies show it costs five times more to gain a new customer than it does to keep an existing one. If you've already won a customer's trust, why not nurture that relationship? Focus on providing exceptional service, upselling complementary products or services, and creating experiences that keep customers coming back, especially the top 20 percent we identified above.

A subscription or recurring revenue model could be a great way to retain customers. When done right, these models provide consistent cash flow and make your business more attractive to buyers.

Expanding Markets: Growth doesn't always mean doing something brand new. Apply the 80/20 Rule to your growth strategy too. Sometimes, it's about taking what's already working and expanding it into a new market. Maybe that's a geographic market, an industry niche, or even a demographic you haven't targeted before.

For example, let's say you run a successful pet care business in one city. Expanding into neighboring cities might be the easiest, fastest way to grow without reinventing the wheel.

Acquisitions: This is one of the most powerful—but often overlooked—ways to grow. Buying another business can give you a fast track to scaling. Why? Because that acquired business can give you instant access to new markets, amazing cross-selling opportunities, new talent and IP, and so much more. It can be especially powerful if your acquisition aligns with the 20 percent of your efforts that drive your biggest wins.

Let's say you own a landscaping company in the suburbs. You find a smaller, struggling company in the same space that operates in a nearby urban market. By acquiring them, you gain access to their customer list, hire their skilled employees, and expand into a new geographic area—without starting from scratch.

Keep in mind that not all growth is good growth. It's easy to fall into the trap of saying yes to every opportunity that comes your way, thinking that more is always better.

But the truth is, saying yes to everything can leave you overstretched and overwhelmed.

The key is to focus on aligned growth—opportunities that match your vision, play to your strengths, and make the most of your resources.

Key Takeaway: Growth isn't about doing more—it's about doing what matters most. Whether you're expanding markets, focusing on customer retention, or exploring acquisitions, the goal is to amplify your success without multiplying your stress.

USE PRODUCTIVE PRESSURE

Once your systems are humming along and your growth strategy is determined, it's time to talk about productive pressure.

This isn't about pushing harder—it's about pushing smarter. It's about applying just enough pressure to create focus, urgency, and results—without tipping over into stress and chaos. Think of it as the accelerator on your growth/scalability engine.

Here are a few ways to leverage productive pressure effectively:

Set Boundaries to Focus Efforts: Growth doesn't happen by accident—it happens when you intentionally focus your energy on what matters most. That means saying no to distractions (even the shiny ones) and setting boundaries around your time, priorities, and resources.

Leverage Constraints to Innovate: Constraints aren't roadblocks—they're tools that force you to clarify what's truly important. Believe it or not, having too much time, money, or freedom can actually hurt your growth. Why? Because constraints are where creativity thrives. When resources are limited, you're forced to think strategically, streamline processes, and innovate in ways you wouldn't otherwise. Constraints, when applied thoughtfully, unlock opportunity.

Create Accountability Loops: We all know that when you set goals and review them, you're more likely to achieve them. The key is consistent check-ins, not micromanagement. Whether it's a team meeting, your progress dashboard, or a quick message, accountability keeps everyone focused and aligned.

Push—but Don't Break: Productive pressure creates balance. You want to push just enough to stretch your team's capabilities and drive results, but not so much that your systems or people start to crack. If you find deadlines slipping, quality dropping, or morale tanking, it's time to recalibrate.

Again, the pressure isn't mean to overwhelm you. Instead, it should drive innovation and help both you and your team to be more efficient and effective.

Key Takeaway: The key to growth and scalability isn't sprinting to the finish line—you want to run a smart, sustainable race. With systems in place and the right amount of productive pressure, you can grow/scale your business without breaking what you've built.

✿ ✿ ✿

The bottom line here is that growth doesn't have to mean chaos. By focusing on building for scalability, pursuing the right opportunities, and applying productive pressure, you *can* hit your goals faster without breaking what you've built.

Everything we have talked about in previous chapters plays into this. If you haven't fixed the fires, reverse engineered your plan, embraced metrics that matter, and made time to work *on* your business instead of *in* your business, it's going to be pretty hard to drive growth.

But don't get discouraged! This is a process. And it takes time. Most business owners I know—including me!—are not the most patient people on planet Earth.

Somehow, we have to maintain a balance between keeping our foot on the gas and realizing that Rome wasn't built in a day. Neither will the ideal version of your business.

The great news is that when you have given attention to these first five keys of the Freedom Flywheel, you'll be set up in an amazing way to tackle the topic of Chapter Seven: Optimize Profitability.

Optimize Profitability

CHAPTER SEVEN

OPTIMIZE PROFITABILITY

Although profitability is the sixth item in the Freedom Flywheel, it's probably the real reason why you're here.

After all, money is the lifeblood of your business. Without profit, you have no freedom—you're stuck in survival mode. You can't pay to hire people, make the pain go away, or even keep the lights on.

If you have profit—and, of course, cash flow—you have leverage. Leverage to take risks. Leverage to grow. Even leverage to step back and enjoy the business you've worked so hard to grow. You can be strategic.

Increased profitability doesn't just mean earning more—it means keeping more of what you already make, using your resources more wisely, and putting your money to work for you.

The easiest place to start is with low-hanging fruit and quick wins.

PROFIT BUCKETS

If your business is a leaky bucket, you want to fix all the leaks. So, before you explore exciting and creative ways to be more profitable, you need to take care of the basics. Any unnecessary costs, inefficiencies, and lost opportunities are draining your hard-earned cash.

There are many ways to do this, but here are a few simple ideas to get you started:

- *Audit Your Subscriptions and Software Licenses:* Organizations often end up with overlapping or underutilized software licenses. Do you really need seven design tools? Cancel any you don't need.

- *Review Vendor Contracts:* Negotiate better terms or find new vendors. I once saved a client $20,000 a year by switching one of their suppliers.

- *Streamline Operations:* If your team is spending hours manually entering data, invest in software to automate it. Yes, it costs up front, but inefficiency is even more expensive.

- *Pay Attention to Energy and Overhead:* Switch to LED lights. Maintain your HVAC. Adjust your thermostat when necessary. Stop printing everything in color. Those small tweaks add up, especially in larger companies.

Once you've plugged the leaks in your bucket, you'll want to turn your attention to the fun stuff ahead in this chapter: *uncovering hidden profit opportunities, turning cash flow into a powerful tool for growth and flexibility,* and *maximizing margins.*

UNCOVER HIDDEN PROFITS

When we think about profitability, we naturally want to look at expenses we can cut. That's typically the first impulse of a business owner who is looking to be more profitable.

I want you to not only plug the leaks but also find sources of revenue you may not have considered before. I call these "revenue gaps." These might be underperforming products or services you either need to improve or discontinue.

We like to hang on to revenue streams because it feels like any income is good income. But just like customers who aren't serving your business well, you can have income streams that aren't serving you well either.

We've all had customers who have cost us too much time and money. The same can be true for some verticals. Maybe you have a whole product line that's underperforming. You tried everything to fix it, but nothing is working.

Painful as it is to admit it, it's probably time to let it go.

Starbucks recently announced that they are trimming back their overcomplicated menu. They were used to adding specialty and seasonal items to the menu without taking anything away. The result was a bloated menu that was increasingly hard to navigate. For every new item added, one more complexity for workers was added, too. They chose to streamline and have discontinued products that don't sell well or have profit margins that are too low.

> **SOMETIMES THE EASIEST WAY TO MAKE MONEY IS TO TAKE SOME THINGS AWAY.**

When you combine that with maximizing your existing revenue, it's a powerful strategy to be more profitable.

Consider doing things like upselling, cross-selling, increasing customer retention, and looking at your pricing strategies. Even small changes in your pricing strategies can make a big difference in your profitability.

Key Takeaway: Take a look at all your current offerings and reduce or get rid of the things that aren't profitable.

TURN CASH FLOW INTO A POWER TOOL

We all know that cash is king!

In many ways, cash flow matters more than revenue. You could be making millions in sales but still be broke if your cash flow is a mess.

This can be a real challenge for seasonal businesses. Their revenue is often concentrated at certain times of the year, but their fixed costs are often year-round. They will have cash surpluses during busy seasons and cash shortages during off-peak times.

This requires excellent cash flow management to avoid straining the company's ability to cover operating costs, maintain inventory, or invest in growth.

Growth is great. Increasing revenue is great. But if you don't have the cash flow to support it, you can get into real trouble. That's why you need to build reserves, so you have a buffer for those lean or uncertain times.

The idea here is to leverage your money wisely and use your profits strategically to fund your growth, but without overextending yourself. In the example I mentioned earlier in the book—where we took on a big client and got into cash flow issues because their payments weren't coming in until three months later—we could have planned better.

My partners and I had taken some distributions out of the company around that time. But in hindsight, we should have left that money in to support the growth.

Cash flow gives you options. You can hire, expand, make improvements, take a vacation, or take distributions without harming the business.

Key Takeaway: Cash flow isn't just a metric; it's your safety net and your growth engine.

MAXIMIZING YOUR MARGINS

The main idea here is that you want to price for profit. Make sure your pricing reflects the value you're delivering.

Many business owners cringe at the thought of raising prices. But that's simply part of doing business. As you offer higher-quality products and services over time, and as your own expertise get sharper, you're offering more value.

Make sure to review all your prices at least annually (if not more frequently). Increasing prices is one of the easiest ways to make more money. Plus, your expenses are always going up, so your prices should too.

Let's look at it from the point of view of a consumer. If you subscribe to streaming services like Netflix, Disney Plus, Hulu, or Max, you are paying more for each of those today than you were two years ago.

Why? Because they have raised prices. Most people just accept those price hikes as a part of life and move on. Some people will cancel if price hikes are too drastic, and they don't perceive additional value. But most people just keep on paying whatever those companies charge.

It's natural to worry that raising prices will cost you customers. The truth is that worry is usually unfounded. It's important to continue to raise your prices to maintain profitability, and also to ensure you can still offer high quality to your customers or clients.

Once you do that, then you want to focus on high-margin activities. It goes back to the 80/20 Rule. Which 20 percent of your products and services are giving you 80 percent of your revenue?

Make sure to look at every measure of profitability across the board. Look at each segment of your business to make sure it's pulling its weight. Just like Starbucks, you might have verticals or product lines that are not serving you. Don't be afraid to get rid of those if they're not profitable.

Key Takeaway: Profitability requires cutting costs and raising prices, which will align your business with what delivers the most value.

✿ ✿ ✿

It may feel a little redundant to say this because we have talked about profitability from so many angles in this book. However, it bears repeating that profitability isn't just about having more money—it's about creating flexibility, stability, and options.

When you uncover hidden profits, master your cash flow, and focus on margins, you can turn your business into a powerful engine for freedom.

We're almost there! Now that we've worked through the first six elements of the Freedom Flywheel, we're ready to tackle the seventh and final one: Multiply Your Value.

Everything has led up to this moment. Turn the page to Chapter Eight to keep going!

Multiply
Your Value

CHAPTER EIGHT

MULTIPLY YOUR VALUE

We're at the final, but arguably most important, part of the Freedom Flywheel journey. If your business was selling your house, this would be a conversation about curb appeal. The key idea of multiplying your value is to create a business that buyers will fall all over themselves to purchase from you.

It means positioning your business as a scalable, attractive asset. People who buy a business are looking to buy an asset. They're not looking to buy a liability or a really expensive job.

Whether you want to sell your business or keep running it, it's important to keep increasing your business's value as the owner. It doesn't matter if you plan on passing it on to your kids, you think you might sell it to some high-level employees, or you're planning on an outside buyer.

Whatever the eventual outcome—and whoever the eventual owner—the most important high-level task you have as a business owner is increasing its value because multiplying its value gives you options.

Most business owners are basing their entire retirement plan on the value of their business. And most financial planners will assign some sort of value to your business based on what you've told them about it, even if it isn't accurate. They will not only be making decisions about how much money you need to retire, they will also be making decisions about your whole investment strategy based on that chunk of money represented by your business. If they believe that money in your business is super secure, they might take more risk with the rest of your portfolio.

There are all sorts of reasons to put as much effort as you can toward multiplying your business's value.

To that end, in this chapter we will look at three strategies for doing that: *focusing on value drivers, building a business buyers want*, and *giving yourself options*.

FOCUS ON VALUE DRIVERS

There are many ways to drive the value of your business. We've already talked about leadership depth, along with the importance of systems and processes to support your growth strategy and allow scalability.

Leadership depth matters because the buyer will want to know the business isn't going to fall apart once you're gone. Well-documented systems ensure the business can run efficiently and not create problems down the road. No potential buyer wants to buy a bunch of headaches.

Let's focus on another vital piece driving value: stable, predictable revenue streams.

A business can have various types of revenue. One of these is what I call "hunted" revenue, basically meaning one-off transactions. This type of revenue requires you to continuously find new customers, and it's also unpredictable and less valuable to buyers. Since there is no guarantee of repeat business, this is generally the least attractive type of revenue.

There are two other types that can radically change your profitability: reoccurring revenue and recurring revenue. They sound similar but are different.

Reoccurring revenue refers to repeat purchases from customers on an irregular schedule, such as event-based or seasonal transactions. This income is somewhat predictable and gives a business some stability.

On the other hand, **recurring revenue** means steady, predictable income from the same customers due to products like subscription services or maintenance contracts. This kind of revenue increases customer retention and loyalty, improves your cash flow, and also happens to be extremely attractive to a potential buyer of your business!

It shouldn't be any surprise that so many purchases have turned into subscription services. It seems like every app or cloud-based service comes with a monthly subscription. It's a great model for businesses and also provides a lot of benefits for customers who can count on updated apps and up-to-date service.

You can think of recurring revenue as the annuity that potential buyers are willing to pay a premium for.

A lot of business owners who have never considered recurring revenue are hesitant to jump into that game. But if you're creative, there are all kinds of ways you can implement this revenue model into your business, especially if you're a service-based business.

Key Takeaway: When a potential buyer is considering your business, they're not looking for headaches—they're looking for a great potential income source. And they're willing to pay more for a business with leadership depth, proven growth strategies, scalable systems, and recurring revenue.

BUILD A BUSINESS BUYERS WANT

When you think about your business from a buyer's perspective, you want to get rid of red flags. These are any risks that could scare off buyers. To go back to the analogy of selling your house, it would be like the buyer pointing out your leaky roof, peeling paint, and the weird smell you've gotten used to.

For your business, one such red flag might be customer concentration. They will ask for your top ten customers, and what percentage of your income comes from those ten. They'll also ask about legal issues like pending or past lawsuits.

You need to have very clean financials, preferably with at least five years of well-documented records. If you think you might sell in five years, you can start working on that now.

The sooner you start working on these things, the easier it will be to sell your business later on. Lots of business owners talk about the nightmare of going through due diligence when selling their business. But it's only a nightmare if you aren't prepared.

If you go through the steps of the Freedom Flywheel, you will be prepared to sell if and when the time comes. You'll already have everything in place. You're basically setting it up as you go.

Back to the main point: You want to eliminate red flags. The fewer headaches a potential buyer sees, the more likely they'll be to pay more. Nobody wants to pay for aggravation.

If you've ever sold your house, you know the pain of trying to fix all those lingering repairs you should have done over the years. You could have saved yourself a lot of heartache if you'd kept up with them.

Business owners are no different. It's easy to let things slide for another six months, a year, or five years because there is no urgency. Then all of a sudden, when you want to sell, you're in panic mode because there's a mountain of work to do.

The other advantage is that if you do this work as you go, you have a much better idea of what you're selling. Why? Because you'll know your business much better. You'll be familiar with every nook and cranny of it.

Going through this process can also give you the opportunity to enhance your brand. A strong brand identity makes your business more desirable. If you have a great reputation and your customers like you, that's a recipe for success. Your business can look great on paper, but you can't fake customer enthusiasm.

All this will also give your business more "curb appeal."

If you've had a growth plan before and you can document that it was successful, that's great. But even if you don't have the energy or desire to grow or scale, if you're well-positioned and can show the potential is there, buyers will love it.

Older business owners may not want to grow or scale, but the younger buyer will love having a plan to follow so that they can. If you can set up your business to appeal to more potential buyers, all the better!

Key Takeaway: Buyers aren't just looking for a business; they're looking for a great opportunity.

GIVE YOURSELF OPTIONS

We've spent a lot of time in this book talking about how to create value for others. But let's not neglect the importance of creating value for you as the owner.

Just like having cash flow gives you options, having a valuable business, built in the way I've described it in this book, gives you options as well.

The idea is that you want to build for freedom both now and in the future. Why? Because a business that's fun to run and highly profitable right *now* is going to be easy to sell and step away from *later*. You always want to have the option of continuing to own it *or* sell it. That way you're in control.

Even if you're not planning to sell anytime soon, you'll want to consider what a potential buyer might want so you can keep your options open. This is similar to building a house with the right number of bedrooms for its *future* buyer in mind.

It's very hard to time the sale of your business for optimal market conditions because they change all the time. But if you're creating value now, you can continue to scale, sell later, or do whatever you want. You simply have more options.

That's why I encourage you to always think like a buyer.

> **A BUSINESS A BUYER WOULD WANT IS A BUSINESS YOU MIGHT WANT TO KEEP!**

A potential buyer will look at your business objectively. Even though you're working in your business day to day, if you follow the principles I've laid out here, you'll be much better equipped to look at your business like a buyer would.

Key Takeaway: The more value you create, the more options you have for selling, scaling, or continuing to enjoy owning your business.

❋ ❋ ❋

As we look toward the end of our journey together, keep this in mind: A valuable business is about numbers and creating something buyers want, while ensuring it can thrive without you.

By focusing on value drivers, while creating a business buyers want, you're not just giving yourself options—you're building freedom. Which is what the journey is about.

Now that you've experienced the whole Freedom Flywheel, in the final chapter I want to challenge you to take action on this material.

It's one thing to read about concepts and understand them. But truly successful business owners don't just learn—they implement and execute. I can't wait to show you the next steps to continue your journey to freedom—whatever that means to you!

ARE YOU
READY TO FLY?

If you were born before the year 2000, you probably have fond memories of playing the classic *Mouse Trap* board game.

The goal of the game was to collect six pieces of "cheese" (cardboard cheese, of course). But the real fun of the game came when it was your turn to pull back the red lever to set the steel marble in motion.

A player turns a crank, turning gears and pushing on a red lever. The lever knocks a stop sign into a green shoe, which kicks a small bucket holding a metal ball. The ball rolls down some blue stairs and into a rain gutter, and then follows the gutter to bump into the bottom of a vertical rod. The top of the rod has a "helping hand" that bumps a bowling ball, making it fall through a "thing-a-ma-jig" and into a red bathtub, then out of the bathtub and onto a diving board. This catapults a green diver into a washtub, knocking loose a cage suspended from the top of a bumpy rod. The cage rattles down the rod and (hopefully) onto another player's unsuspecting mouse, trapping it. (Notwithstanding the fact that the mouse was made of plastic and not a sentient being in the first place. But I digress.)

Collecting the cheese pieces was just an excuse to watch all these crazy pieces come together to create something fun. So fun, in fact, that the *Mouse Trap* game is now over sixty years old and still a top seller for Hasbro.

Here's the thing, though: the fun of *Mouse Trap* doesn't come automatically. You have to set up the game first.

If you just dump out the pieces onto the floor, they're not going to magically arrange themselves on the board. You have to follow the directions and make sure it's all set up the way the designer intended.

Sure, it takes a bit of time to set up. But once it's ready, then the real fun can begin.

In the same way, the Freedom Flywheel takes some time to set up, but the results are well worth it! It creates that same kind of momentum, setting off a chain reaction of profitability, scalability, and greater potential than you can imagine.

In this book, you have learned how to create FREEDOM by implementing the key components of the Flywheel:

- **F**ix the Fires
- **R**everse Engineer Your Plan
- **E**mbrace Metrics That Matter
- **E**stablish Owner Independence
- **D**rive Growth and Scalability
- **O**ptimize Profitability
- **M**ultiply Your Value

I've done my best to make the Freedom Flywheel as simple and streamlined as possible by focusing on these seven elements.

As we talked about earlier in the book, a flywheel is a mechanical device that's designed to store energy and create momentum. When you apply this concept to the world of business, it's a collection of interdependent elements that work together in a system to create momentum, power, and success.

When you integrate the concepts of the Freedom Flywheel into *your* business, you get far more momentum, efficiency, profitability, and—perhaps most importantly—FUN!

I don't want your journey to end here at the end of this book. In fact, this is only the beginning! I want to invite you to work with me to put these principles into practice and start seeing amazing results.

FREEDOM IS WORTH IT

As a veterinarian, I've seen what happens when potential is wasted. A horse bred to win races can't succeed if it doesn't get the care and training it needs.

The same is true for your business. Without the right systems and strategy, it's easy to fall short of what's possible.

Making big changes in your business will never feel convenient. Life is always busy, and there will always be a reason to put it off. But the longer you wait, the harder it gets to catch up.

It's easy to think, *I'll fix this later*, but "later" rarely shows up when we expect it to. Instead of waiting, what if you started taking action today? When you do, you'll not just be investing in your business—you'll be investing in your future self.

Today I encourage you to consider what your future could be like a few years down the road. Do you want to own a booming, profitable business, knowing you made the changes that were needed? Or do you want to be weighed down by the regret that you didn't take action when you had the opportunity?

> **THERE'S NEVER A GOOD TIME TO MAKE CHANGES. LIFE GETS IN THE WAY. WE'RE BUSY. THERE'S ALWAYS TOO MUCH ON OUR PLATE.**

But as the old saying goes, the best time to plant a tree was twenty years ago. The second-best time is *today*.

Imagine a life where your business runs like a well-oiled machine, your team thrives, and you have the time and energy to focus on what matters most. That's what the Freedom Flywheel can give you.

When you implement the Freedom Flywheel, you're not just putting business systems in place. You're creating the life you truly want.

I've been where you are—busy, over-committed, and wondering if things would ever change. I'm living proof that they can. I've walked down this path myself, and I love helping others walk it too.

Now it's *your* turn.

I can understand if you are feeling a little overwhelmed. It's true that each of these steps can be daunting. You don't have to do it alone. The most successful business owners know when to ask for help—and that's where I come in.

Are you ready to stop being owned by your business and start owning your future? We can get started on your journey today, together.

Let's have a conversation to see if we're a great fit.

If you've made it this far, you already have the tools to transform your business. But let's not stop here. Transformation happens when you take action.

I want to personally invite you to work with me to implement the Freedom Flywheel in your business. Together, we can fast-track your results and create the freedom you deserve.

Visit ProductivePressure.com/Flywheel to connect with me and get this book's bonuses.

WOULD YOU REVIEW THIS BOOK?

If you enjoyed reading *The Business Owner's Freedom Flywheel*, would you kindly take a few moments to leave a review wherever you purchased it (and perhaps even Goodreads.com)? I'm grateful for your support. Thank you!

GRATITUDE

Writing a book is a little like running a business—you think you're in charge, but really, you're only as strong as the people around you. I've had an incredible team of supporters, encouragers, and idea-bouncers who have made this book (and quite frankly, my life) infinitely better.

First and foremost, to my husband Bob—thank you for always believing in me, no matter how many squirrels and shiny things I chase. Seriously, if I woke up tomorrow and decided to start an alpaca farm on Mars, you'd probably just nod, ask how you can help, and remind me to bring a good coat.

To my kids—Jack, for always making time to talk through my latest ideas and then dropping those sharp insights that make me go, "Why didn't I think of that?" And Emma, for your laser-focused attention to detail and willingness to slog through pages of my ramblings to give feedback that makes my thoughts make sense on paper. You two are the best volunteer editors ever!

To my clients—working with you has shown me that while these concepts might seem simple, they're far from easy. Your willingness to answer the tough questions, do the hard things, and make shit happen is what made me realize: This stuff matters. It's hard to see your own blind spots, and even harder to admit when you need help. That's why this framework exists—not to judge, but to give you a roadmap from where you are now to where you actually want to be. Thank you for trusting me to help you on that journey.

And finally, to my rockstar book team— Honorée Corder, Kent Sanders, MJ James, Alyssa Archer, Mike McConnell, and Dino Marino. You took on all the things so I didn't have to, which meant I could stay in my lane, do what I do best, and leave the rest to the pros. This book exists because of your expertise, patience, and ability to see the method to my madness.

To everyone who has supported, encouraged, or even just listened to me ramble about business strategy at inappropriate times—thank you. This book is for you.

ABOUT THE AUTHOR

Dawn Bloomer is a Business & Exit Planning Strategist who helps entrepreneurs build businesses that are fun to run now and easy to sell later. A former veterinarian-turned-business advisor, Dawn has been on both sides of the buyer-seller equation—and learned a lot along the way.

She bought into a well-established business, convinced she could make it better (despite having zero formal business training at the time). Years (and many wins and losses) later, she and her partner merged their practice into a larger group. From there, Dawn helped identify other businesses to buy to expand that group—until they were ultimately acquired by a much larger, private equity backed, aggregator. Along the way, she experienced firsthand the pain of due diligence, the challenges of post-transaction transitions, and the hard lessons that come from doing things the wrong way before figuring out how to do them right.

Now, as a Certified Exit Planning Advisor (CEPA) and MBA, Dawn helps business owners avoid the common pitfalls she's seen (and lived). She knows that building a business that runs smoothly without the owner at the center isn't always easy—it takes the right structure, strategy, and mindset—not to mention, hard work. That's why she created the Freedom Flywheel™ framework—to help business owners do it faster, with fewer headaches, and more clarity so they can have fun and freedom now, not just later.

When she's not helping business owners unlock the value in their companies, Dawn can be found having fun with her family, traveling, sailing, or pursuing another technology rabbit hole!

For more insights and resources, visit www.productivepressure.com or connect with Dawn on LinkedIn.

www.ingramcontent.com/pod-product-compliance
Lightning Source LLC
Chambersburg PA
CBHW071424210326
41597CB00020B/3637